# A PORTRAIT OF
# BACH

# A PORTRAIT OF

# BACH

*by* JO MANTON

*Illustrated by Faith Jacques*

ABELARD-SCHUMAN
New York

TO

THE BACH CHOIR OF LONDON

# TABLE OF CONTENTS

# LIST OF ILLUSTRATIONS

## AUTHOR'S NOTE

THIS book tries to give an honest picture of a great man and his life.

From his childhood until almost the day of his death Sebastian Bach was a practical musician, with no time to write letters except on professional affairs. Fortunately his sons and pupils valued all that he told them in the course of his teaching and remembered much of it to tell to his first biographer, Johann Nicolaus Forkel. There is therefore some evidence for everything that Bach says in this book, though not always for his exact words.

The descriptions of his family, and of the persons and places in his life, are also true, thanks to the research of generations of scholars, above all to Bach's classic biographers, Spitta, Schweitzer, and Terry, and to Karl Geiringer, the historian of the Bach family. All lovers of music owe them gratitude for opening to us the world of Bach.

The poems and letters by J. S. Bach quoted in this book are drawn from the following sources: *Bach: A Biography* by C. S. Terry (Oxford University Press, London and New York, 1928), *A Bach Reader* by H. J. David and A. Mendel (J. M. Dent, London, 1946, and W. W. Norton Co., New York, 1945), *Bach* by Esther Meynell (Duckworth, London, 1936, and A. A. Wyn, New York). The poem on page 87 was translated by Robert Gittings, who also read the book in proof and made many valuable suggestions.

# CHAPTER ONE

# A FAMILY OF MUSICIANS

## (1685-1691)

The house of Johann Ambrosius Bach, court musician to Duke Georg and town musician to the city of Eisenach, stood in a wide cobbled street. As they rounded the corner on their way home from religious school, Jakob and Sebastian Bach could see the red roof, the kitchen chimney, black with smoke, and the three windows of the attic where the apprentices slept side by side upon the floor.*

They ran across the grass plot and pushed at the heavy double doors, which swung slowly open into the dark archway. It was now 1691, but the inside of the house had not changed much since the Middle Ages. The boys stood in a passage of worn bricks, with black-beamed walls and ceiling, which led through to the inner courtyard and the garden. On one side an oak staircase rose to the living rooms above; on the other a door opened into the dim spaces of the barn. Here their mother dried herbs and

---

*There is a strong tradition in Eisenach that Johann Sebastian was born in the house which has long been the Bach museum. Some scholars now think that he was born in another old house nearby, which has since been destroyed.

stored logs for the winter; here Sebastian, forever curious about sounds, could try his voice among the echoing rafters, and here the boys could play in wet weather, free to shout and scuffle as much as they liked, without disturbing their father at his work.

Now, as they opened the door, the whole house seemed to wake and murmur like a living thing. From upstairs, where the big music room looked down over the garden, came a hum of voices; then silence, followed by the sound of violins and cellos tuning.

"Lesson or rehearsal?" asked Jakob, and stood in the passage listening.

"One, two, three, and—!" cried their father's voice from above. The strings struck up, then faltered and died away. Sebastian could picture his father as he had so often seen him, shirt open at the neck, old brown working coat thrown around his shoulders, and one shapely hand raised in the conductor's gesture of command.

"One!" cried his father again, and struck the harpsichord. The notes, crisp and light as frosty leaves, came dancing down the stairs towards them. Led by his playing, the strings took up their tune.

"Rehearsal," said Jakob, "and they need it! But listen, that harpsichord has a good true note since Father and I tuned it."

"The clavier has more sweetness," said Sebastian, with the determination of his six years holding its own against a brother of nine.

"Clavier! What's the use of an instrument no one can hear except the fellow who's playing it?" said Jakob.

Sebastian scowled. In matters of music he would never

*From upstairs came the sound of violins and cellos tuning.*
*(A corner of the staircase in the Bach Museum*
*at Eisenach.)*

give way to anybody. He knew that he would always love the soft but sweet-voiced clavier above all keyboard instruments. Jakob imitated his lowering look until they caught each other's eye, and both burst out laughing.

"Sh!" said Jakob. "You know Father doesn't allow us to make a noise during rehearsals."

The violins held the air now, while the cellos laid a strong ground bass and the tender violas wove a web of sound between. The paneled walls and staircase re-echoed the sound. The Bachs' house was awake, alive with music. They were a family of musicians born and bred. At any time of day the sound of violins, trumpets, and kettledrums rang through their home. Today it was a string band rehearsing for the Duke's birthday festival. Tomorrow it might be a party of friends to play quartets in the evenings, or a choir rehearsing for a wedding. Always there would be music.

After the rehearsal it was time for Sebastian's regular lesson. Ambrosius Bach lifted his youngest son onto the clavier stool, and laid cushions upon the family Bible until the little boy could spread his hands upon the keys. Their father had already taught three older sons the family craft. Christoph, the oldest, had gone into the world to earn his living as an organist; Balthasar was a court trumpeter; and Jakob, who was still at school, already showed promise as an oboe player. Yet of all his sons none was so quick, so naturally a musician, as this youngest. There seemed to be an inherited sureness in his hands as he touched the keys, or felt his way delicately along the fingerboard of the violin.

Music was the earliest sound Sebastian could remember. It had started before his conscious memory, while he still rocked in the wooden cradle beside the great four-poster bed. The sound of playing and singing took its place with the ring of the axe on wood in the courtyard, or the clatter of cooking pots on the brick oven. He heard his mother calling for more logs to fill the great hearth, wide as a blacksmith's forge, and in the same moment his father's voice from the music room, "Again, from the beginning." Before he could understand it, he grew to expect the enchantment that followed.

Sebastian learned notes with his first words, and written music with his alphabet. Now, at six, he could copy, play, or hear two or three interlaced lines of melody as naturally as one listens in a room where several voices are talking.

The lesson went on through scales, exercises, ear training and reading from a bass part with only figures to show the notes above. Sebastian listened for his father's correction or his rare words of praise. Ambrosius Bach never boasted to the world of his son's talents, and Sebastian was never forced into being an infant prodigy. The only comment that his father made was at the end of the lesson, when the shadows began to gather in the room and Sebastian's sister came in with the heavy pewter candlesticks. Then he stood up, closed the clavier and said, "You have made progress, my son. It is time to think of organ lessons. Tomorrow you go to Uncle Christoph."

Uncle Christoph was a fine organist and composer who directed the music of the great St. George's Church in Eisenach. His fame was one of the chief glories of the Bach family, and to be taught by him, even occasionally, was an honor indeed. Sebastian knew it well.

"Yes, Father," he said.

Next day Jakob took his hand and led him through the farm wagons and stalls to St. George's Church. Together they climbed the long dark ladder to the organ loft, high on the western wall.

"Come, boy; sit here beside me," said Uncle Christoph,

turning back the full skirts of his coat to make room. Sebastian climbed onto the narrow bench, his legs dangling in space. Uncle Christopher set up a well-thumbed manuscript on the organ desk before him.

"Now watch me," he said, "and when I nod, like this—" his curled gray wig jerked sharply—"turn over. Never move until I give the signal, and never put your fingers over the notes."

Sebastian watched with patient concentration while his uncle played, and Jakob toiled at the foot-bellows. Soon he could follow the tiny, sharply scratched notes in the manuscript before him and anticipate the turn-over.

"Good," said Uncle Christoph briefly. "Now you may stand beside me and pull the stops when I tell you."

The organ rang out into the great bare church with triumphant authority. Sometimes the notes were high and bright as a trumpet, sometimes deep as the march of a far-off army. Sebastian pulled the stops and noted in his memory how the tones and colors of the music seemed to blend at his touch. The two candles lighting the dark loft wavered, burned down, guttered in their sockets. He did not notice the passing of time.

From this day onwards he had occasional organ lessons with his uncle, as well as regular training at home. The organ loft took its place naturally in his life, with his father's rehearsals, and the winter evenings when they sang by the light of the kitchen fire.

Music was already Sebastian's chosen language, and so it would be, till the end of his life.

# CHAPTER TWO

# FAMILY GATHERING

## (1691-1693)

Once a year the Bach household was turned upside down. It began as a murmur in garret and barn: "The cousins are coming!"

The murmur swelled to a fine crescendo as Frau Bach began to stir in her kitchen and storerooms. A pig was killed; hams and sausages hung smoking in the wide chimney; smoke rose from the brewhouse and a tantalizing scent came from the bread oven. Tubs of salt beef and pickled herrings were rolled into the barn. Sebastian's two older sisters and the servant fell to scrubbing, polishing, and laundering. The whole house shone and the family stood ranged in spotless shirts and aprons, waiting for the rumble of wagons on the cobbles outside, and the cry, "The cousins are here!"

The Bachs were an immense family, with many branches spreading through the towns of their native Thuringia and further afield. Whatever happened in the world outside, it was their custom to hold a gathering of the whole family every year, often at Eisenach. Perhaps because they were all musicians, they held fast to each other all their lives.

"In our town," said Uncle Christian of Erfurt proudly,

19

"they call all musicians Bachs. Our family has given its name to the craft."

The wagons rolled into the yard one by one, and the children ran out to welcome their visitors. Talk and laughter bubbled up, with all the excitement of a year's news to exchange, until old Uncle Heinrich of Arnstadt silenced them, hand uplifted.

"Children, have you no reverence? God's service before man's service!"

Then, just as they had started their day's work with prayer, they started their feast with a hymn, standing soberly around the table to sing the four-square harmonies of Luther which they knew and loved so well.

They sat down with a scrape of benches and a cheerful rattle of knives and forks. They clashed the tankards of beer and shouted, "A health to us all! A very good health!" The family likeness among them, the sense of a tribe, was almost overwhelming; but to the boys at Eisenach each branch seemed to bring its own spirit to the gathering. Uncles Christoph, Ernst, Heinrich, and Johannes were all organists, with something of the dignity of the Lutheran service clinging to their black coats and powdered wigs. The cousins from Gotha and Meiningen were town and court musicians, bringing a lilting gaiety and elegance from their evening concerts. If the boys had a favorite, it was their orphan cousin Maria Barbara, with her fresh young voice and her cheeks glowing beneath her starched white cap.

The children sat at table with their elders, all but the babies who were stowed away in cots and cradles upstairs. Crowded on the narrow benches, eyes sparkling and cheeks flushed with excitement, the boys drained their tankards of small beer, while the girls ran to and from the kitchen for dishes of festive carp, veal, and huge pink hams. Old family jokes, stories of childhood long since forgotten, flew around the table, and the family laugh, deep and ringing, echoed from the paneled walls.

No one would have thought, to see the Bachs at their family table, that in the lifetime of many of them Germany had suffered thirty years of disastrous war. Cities had burned down, great lords and their castles had been destroyed, but the Bachs had come through it all, unchanged. Half peasant, half craftsman, each had tilled his fields and practiced his music while the great world thundered by outside. If the children asked for a story of old times it was not of the war that the uncles told, but of the family, and the first of their name.

"Veit Bach, your great-great-grandfather was called, boys. He was a miller, grinding corn by a stream for his living, but he loved music and used to take his zither in to the mill, and play it while the great grindstones turned."

"A pretty noise the pair of them must have made," thought Sebastian. "But perhaps the pounding of the mill taught him to keep time."

"Please, Grandfather, show us Hans the Fiddler," begged Maria Barbara, and the children crowded around the engraved picture of a bearded man, with jester's cap and forelock, holding a tiny fiddle.

"What relation he was, exactly, I do not know," said the old man, "but he was a court jester. Look, you can read the rhyme above the picture:

Here at his fiddling see Hans Bach!
Whatever he plays, he makes you laugh;
For he scrapes away in a style all his own,
And wears a fine beard by which he is known!"

"So he was a musician, too?" asked Jakob.

"Yes," said old Heinrich, "since old Veit we have all
been musicians, each following his craft, giving thanks
to God and owing nothing to any man."

Sooner or later one of the children would shout, "Now
a song! A quodlibet!"

"Very well," said Ambrosius from the head of the table.
"A quodlibet, or what you will!"

They all began to sing at once, each one a different

*"Now a song! A quodlibet!"*

song of his or her own choice, shouting out the words of love ballads or drinking songs, and trying not to catch each other's eyes. Somehow, since they were all musicians, the tangle of sound twisted into one harmonious skein, unless they broke down before the end in uproarious laughter. Passers-by in the street could not help stopping to listen, and laughing too. As the flood of sound rolled from the window, the citizens of Eisenach said to each other, "The Bachs are having a party again." It was late at night before the last candles were blown out, and they climbed the stairs. Even then the children, packed three in a bed, would laugh and whisper until morning.

# CHAPTER THREE

## "HERE FIND MUSIC"

### (1693-1695)

Although music kept all the Bachs indoors a good deal, there was nothing confined or unnatural about Sebastian's boyhood. Eisenach was a city of market-town size, sheltered within its medieval walls under the flank of a steep hills. From church towers and attics one could see the peaks of the Thuringian Forest, whose mountains were covered with mile upon mile of green pinewoods where the woodman's axe and the huntsman's horn were the only human sounds to be heard. On the other side of the city the arched gateways led out to a green plain where oxen ploughed a long furrow across the hedgeless fields. The villages were scattered, each a few cottages, with a whitewashed church in the center. Within the walls of Eisenach itself, three hills thrust steeply upwards, dwarfing the church spires below. On the highest of them a stately castle, the Wartburg, towered over the little city, like a picture in a fairy tale.

Sebastian must often have climbed the path to the Wartburg, at first with an older brother or friend to tell him its many stories.

"This is the castle to which Martin Luther was taken

when he defied the Pope and the Emperor in open council
and lay under sentence of death. As he rode home from
the council meeting at Worms, friends ambushed him in
a lonely wood and brought him safely into hiding here.
This is the very room in which he lived for months. Here
he translated the Latin Bible into our own German tongue,
and here he composed his hymns."

"The very same ones that we sing on Sundays and holy
days? The ones Uncle Christoph plays?"

"Yes, here, in this very room."

They looked round the vaulted stone chamber, and
out over the roofs of the town. It seemed to bring their
church very near to their everyday lives.

From the time Sebastian was eight years old, the boys
were off in the morning soon after daybreak, since school
began at six in summer and seven in winter. In sunshine
or snow, there was just time to swallow the old German
breakfast of beer and black bread, before they ran out into the street. Past the gabled house where Luther had once
lodged they cluttered, along a leafy avenue, by the palace
in the market place where their father's employer, Duke
Johann Georg, lived, past the church where Uncle Christoph
was preparing to play for morning service, and over the
square to school.

Eisenach Gymnasium, or Grade School, was housed
in the buildings of an old monastery, dissolved at the Reformation. Now boys ran races around the cloisters where
the monks had paced, and played games in the flagged
courtyard. In the cold refectory and dormitories Sebastian
mastered his early lessons. This meant pages of learning
by heart German and Latin in parallel columns, reading

*The gymnasium at Eisenach*

the Gospels and Epistles in heavy volumes of black German type, or reciting Luther's Catechism and the Psalms. The work was not easy for a child, and no one had thought of making it pleasant, but the Bachs had a tradition of hard work behind them and Sebastian had a good brain. At nine years old he stood higher in class then Jakob, who was twelve. His letters in later life show that he had a good all-round education, and when he became a schoolmaster he was to teach Latin as well as music.

Morning school at Eisenach ended at nine or ten, and the afternoon lessons were from one until three, with Wednesday and Saturday as half-holidays. Jakob and Sebastian did not have all this free time for their own amusement, though, for naturally, as the Town Musician's sons, they were both in the choir. This boy's choir was the pride of both the school and the city. Dr. Andreas Dedekind, the master who conducted it, lost no chance of teaching the young singers their responsibility.

He stood on the dais, impressive in his black Cantor's gown. "The very name of our city, boys, speaks of music. Eisenach, in Latin Isenacum; that is to say, 'en musica,' or in the German, 'here find music.' Likewise in Isenacum may we read 'en canimus' meaning . . . ."

He would look around the room and pounce on some unlucky idler. "Meaning—?"

"We are singing!" shouted a chorus of forty boys, eager to shorten the lecture and escape into the sunshine.

"Indeed we see this is a name most justly earned," continued the Cantor, unrelenting. "Here in our stately Wartburg the minstrels of the Middle Ages held their Tourney of Song. Here, in this very choir, the great Luther sang. Be sure that you are worthy of your inheritance."

The Eisenach choir, under Dr. Dedekind, was famous throughout Thuringia, which has always been a land of singers. Yet even in this excellent choir the small Sebastian Bach was outstanding, and listeners spoke of his "rarely beautiful soprano voice."

Every Sunday the forty choristers, soberly dressed in black gowns and white ruffs, filed into the gallery of St. George's Church to sing the long Lutheran morning service while Uncle Christoph Bach played the organ in the loft overhead. At weddings and funerals the singers were paid a fee, and Sebastian could come home proudly with a silver penny in his breeches pocket. For most of their pocket money, though, the boys relied upon "Currenden."

These Currenden were a custom which had grown up over centuries. At regular seasons of the year the boys filed through the streets two by two, stopping every now and again to sing and collect pennies from the passers-by. At New Year, and in spring or summer, they sometimes went out into the nearby villages to show their skill to the peasants. While the long evenings faded into an opal twilight, they would sing until the last ox cart had gone creaking home with the last load of hay, and the village goosegirl had driven her hissing flock into their pen for the night. Sometimes they made their way home by the light of the moon.

When Sebastian was eight years old the School Rector decided these country wanderings were harmful to discipline and forbade them. He relented only when the boys presented him with an impressive petition in Latin, beginning, *"Te etiam atque oramus"*:

"We pray you that of your benevolence you will permit us to sing in the villages round about. Necessity prompts us to do this, as our intention is to buy books."

What headmaster could refuse this? There is no record, though, that the boys bought any books in the end.

At winter festivals, the Feast of Stephen or the Holy Innocents, the choir sang its way through the streets and squares of the city. The people of Eisenach loved their boys' choir. When they heard the muffled tramp of feet and saw the red glow of torches upon the snow, they would open their shutters, wincing a little at the frosty air, but eager for the sound of the fresh young voices.

"O little one sweet, O little one mild,
The Father's purpose thou hast fulfilled."

The soprano voices soared up to the snowy rooftops
and beyond, as though their singing would reach to the
stars. All his life Sebastian Bach remembered the chorales
he had sung as a chorister, and set them repeatedly to rich
and tender harmonies.

Winter brought with it, too, the joys of the Christmas
fair. Braziers of charcoal glowed upon the trodden snow,
and the streets were crammed with booths and handcarts.
The peasants cried their wares from every village around:
carved wooden toys from Sonneberg, pipe-bowls from
Ohrdruf, lutes and zithers from Kräwinkle, and the sharp-
scented "Christ-trees" from the depths of the forest.

This joyous childhood lasted only ten years. In May,
1694, Sebastian lost his mother, while she was still a young
woman. She was worn out, perhaps, by the strenuous
work of a large household. Sudden death was a common-
place of the age, and mourning, however deep, could not
last long. A few months later Ambrosius Bach married
again—the widow of a clergyman, who came to take up
the reins of the household, bringing a little stepsister for
the Bach children.

Sebastian and Jakob returned to school. Their sisters
took up their scrubbing and polishing and laundry work
under Frau Barbara's direction. It seemed as though life,
though deprived of a beloved voice and hand, might still
go on.

Two months later, in January 1695, the season of the
chief Currenden, perhaps even while the boys, lantern

over shoulder, were singing their New Year's hymn, the summons came.

"Jakob and Sebastian Bach—to your home at once!"

They ran along the streets which had so often echoed to their tread. At the house door they met the pastor of St. George's Church. He carried the vessels for Holy Communion, and looked gravely at them as they hurried past.

Their kindly stepmother, Frau Barbara, ran down the stairs to meet them, wringing her hands in her apron.

"My children, your father, your good father—!"

Sebastian Bach was an orphan indeed.

# CHAPTER FOUR

# THE BROTHERS

## (1695-1700)

Ambrosius Bach was buried in the bitter cold of February 1695. His oldest son, who had left home, returned to follow his father's body to the snow-filled churchyard and the younger children huddled forlornly around the grave.

Jakob and Sebastian took their places in the choir and sang the funeral psalms. They took what comfort they could from the familiar melodies and sang, as their father would have wished, carefully, their eyes fixed on the Cantor and the roll of music with which he beat time. Whatever changed in their lives, music still remained.

The Eisenach household was now finally broken up. One sister was old enough to be married. Frau Barbara, who may have had a little property, took the other to bring up with her own child. There remained Jakob and Sebastian, still a month short of his tenth birthday. Their stepmother could hardly accept so heavy a charge; more important, she could not train the two boys in their hereditary family craft.

The head of the family was now Johann Christoph, who was twenty-four and earned a meager living as a

village organist at Ohrdruf. He presided over a family
council in the half-dismantled house, and announced his
decision.

"There is nothing else for it. The boys must come
home with me."

Coach travel in those days was a luxury for the rich.
Jakob and Sebastian covered the thirty miles to Ohrdruf
in a farm cart, pulled by two oxen. There was room beside
the driver for Johann Christoph, but the two boys had to
sit among straw, upon the wooden chest that held the
whole of their possessions. They traveled most of the day
across a wide moor, where springs of water bubbled among
the snowy heather. In spite of the straw it was bitingly
cold. Towards evening they turned into the hills, winding
through lovely glens and valleys, through forests of pine
and fir. The early winter darkness was drawing in when
they reached a walled village of cobbled streets and
gabled houses in the heart of the Thuringerwald. They
crossed a shallow mountain stream which brawled its way
through the market place, and turned in at a narrow
street by the church. At last the cart drew up before a
very small cottage. Christoph lifted out his small brother,
cramped and stiff with hours of jolting, and set him down
before the door. This house was to be Sebastian's home
for the next five years.

Johann Christoph had married, only a few months
before a young girl of Ohrdruf, and they were now ex-
pecting their first child. What must Dorothea Bach have
felt when she saw her home invaded by these two
strangers? Jakob, only a few years younger than herself,
was at the hobbledehoy age. She looked from him to the

younger child, and saw a sturdy, thickset boy with broad brow, determined jaw and wide open, steady eyes which seemed fixed upon some vision of his own. She could not help having a sinking feeling at the cares which lay ahead, but the Bach family tradition was overriding. Without a word of complaint to the outside world, the young couple set about making a home for their brothers.

The Bachs believed in good education and, poor as they were, Jakob and Sebastian were sent at once to the village school beside the church. By a happy chance Ohrdruf school was famous for its teaching, and three hundred boys gathered there from nearby villages. The Duke of Saxe-Gotha, who was patron of the school, made education his hobby, and Sebastian was only the most gifted of many boys who enjoyed his experiments. At Ohrdruf there were interesting lessons, books the boys could enjoy reading, and masters who treated them as friends. Sebastian went through school easily, always two years ahead of his age, and confidently faced tests each year in writing, arithmetic, divinity, Latin and Greek, science and geography—unusual subjects in those days—and, of course, in music. It was a well-balanced education for a boy whose genius was to grow from balance and sanity. One lover of Bach's music, Esther Meynell, has put this very well. She wrote, "He is like a great tree, his boughs waving high among the stars, while his roots are imbedded deeply in the wholesome earth."

Ohrdruf school had its own choir of thirty voices which, like the Eisenach choir, made Currenden at the New Year, and in March, July, and October. Sebastian, although he was only ten, knew how short money was in his brother's house. Here was a chance to pay his own way in life and be independent, at least in part. At the first opportunity he went in for the choir auditions, when his fine treble voice and quickness at reading music at once won him a place among the sopranos. Now he listened with a seriousness beyond his years to the clink of coins in the choir collection bag. At the end of each year the boys lined up to receive their share of the collection— from seventeen thalers (about $20) for a first year boy to twenty for a leader. After the pay parade there was a rush to the pastry shop for a meat tart in winter, or summer's cherry tarts. Some boys, more thrifty, saved their earnings in a clay pig for some future treat. Sebastian's share went straight home to be converted into salt herrings, firewood, or shoe leather. During the five years he lived under Christoph's roof, he must almost have paid for his keep.

The boys probably helped the household in other ways as well. Tradition is strong in Germany against men doing women's work, but Dorothea was certainly too poor to employ a household servant. Sebastian must have cleaned shoes, split the logs, and carried the sacks of corn which formed part of his brother's salary. When a succession of babies appeared, to fill the house with their lusty yells, the twelve-year-old uncle probably had to take his turn at rocking the cradle, or sailing paper boats on the tumbling waters of the Ohra.

In return, Christoph gave Sebastian not only a home but a thorough musical training. The week filled up with regular lessons in organ, clavier, and composition. Christoph had been placed by his father as pupil to a great organist, and he passed on his master's teaching with patience and thoroughness.

The organ is built to speak with many voices at once, and so it satisfies the keenest ear and brain. Sebastian took to it as a swan to the water. In his own lifetime he was chiefly famous as an organist, and the foundations of his mastery were laid at Ohrdruf by his brother.

Yet even this thorough teaching was not enough to satisfy his eager mind. In clavier and harmony he wanted to press on beyond the limits that Christoph would allow. Hardly had he been set one piece to learn than he was back again at his brother's elbow.

"I know it, Christoph. I can play it by heart, without the music! Give me another piece, more difficult this time."

Christoph looked thoughtful.

"Please, Christoph, let me learn a piece from the big book you keep locked up in the cupboard!"

The book was a collection of manuscripts, copied from the most famous composers of the day. It was one of Christoph's most treasured possessions.

"No, Sebastian, not yet. You are not ready for it yet." Christoph felt that he must control this restless pupil.

Sebastian returned to the attack next day, and the next, with all the Bach obstinacy. But Christoph was also a Bach, and having made up his mind would not go back on it. He could not guess the plan that was forming in his young brother's mind.

"You look tired, Sebastian. How red and swollen your eyes are! Finish your supper quickly and go to bed," said Dorothea a few days later.

"Please may I have a candle?" asked Sebastian.

"A candle in your bedroom! Whatever put such an idea into your head? You know we cannot afford luxuries of that sort!"

Sebastian said nothing, and in a few days he looked less tired; but the next month there he was again, yawning and frowning, with red-rimmed eyes.

On dark nights he slept, having nothing better to do, but whenever there was a glimmer of moonlight at the window he forced himself to stay awake, with Jakob snoring by his side. He listened for the church clock, the creak of the stairs, the sound of the baby stirring and being comforted, the final closing of the bedroom door. Then, holding his breath, he stole down barefoot. The familiar rooms looked strangely flat and colorless in the moonlight. A silver ray danced on the music room floor and the copying desk by the window; the open harpsichord threw a menacing wing of shadow on the wall. Sebastian curled up his small supple hand and eased it through the lattice-front of the cupboard. The darkness seemed waiting to pounce on him, as he rolled the sheet of music and drew it out. He spread it on the table and began to copy it, stealthily and fast. The flickering shadows strained his eyes, his heart thumped every time a sleeper stirred upstairs, yet he did not give up. In six months' toil he copied the whole book.

To play the forbidden pieces was a fearful joy. He touched them softly on the clavichord, head bent over the keyboard to catch the last delicate vibration, yet alert for his brother's footstep on the stair.

The day came when Christoph, hearing an unexpected

*Whenever there was a glimmer of moonlight...*

melody, flung open the door and found his young brother with the copy open before him.

"Where did you get that?" he demanded furiously. "You stole it!"

Sebastian's eyes flashed; all through his life he was jealous of his own honor.

"I am not a thief! I copied it myself!"

"Give it to me at once!" Christoph was really angry; a master's authority over his apprentice was complete and not to be questioned. He slammed the copy into a chest and turned the key.

"But the music," thought Sebastian defiantly, "the real music is here, in my head. No one can take that away from me."

The two brothers were both hot-tempered, and they must have been very angry with each other, but we can be sure they made it up. Bach family feeling was stronger than anything else. Sebastian dedicated one of his earliest clavier pieces to his brother and teacher, while Christoph named one of his little sons Sebastian. Their two families were still close friends years later.

Nevertheless, when he was fourteen years old, Sebastian left Ohrdruf, never to return. At his birthday he had been confirmed, which in those days meant he was ready to earn his own living. Jakob had already gone back to Eisenach to be apprenticed to an organist there. Sebastian felt it was time to go out into the world and make his own way as a man. He found a good friend to advise him in his school music master, Elias Herda.

"When I was your age," said Herda, "I had a choral scholarship at the choir school of St. Michael's Church in Lüneburg. That is the place for a musician to learn his craft! There you have the best teachers, a fine standard of performance in the choir, and a chance to hear the greatest organists in Germany. Buxtehude is at Lubeck, Reinken at Hamburg, and Böhm at Lüneburg itself. You could have lessons from him."

"I would give anything to hear them all." The boy's eyes shone with pleasure. "I must go. But will they take me in the choir without a trial?"

"They will always take a Thuringian on trust," said Herda. "They call ours the country of singing birds. I will give you an introduction to the Cantor at St. Michael's. But how will you travel there? It is two hundred miles— a fortune on the coach!"

Sebastian looked sober; he was considering the cost of the journey, and wondering what he could hope to earn. Herda studied the boy who stood before him—the stocky figure, the shabby coat, the steady, far-seeing eyes.

"With God's help you will succeed," he said. He knew that here was a boy who would fight his way through any difficulties.

# CHAPTER FIVE

# CHORISTER SEBASTIAN BACH

## (1700-1703)

Sebastian set off on a wild March day in the year 1700, to begin a new life with the new century. A school companion, Georg Erdmann, traveled with him, also bound for Lüneburg and St. Michael's choir. The two boys set their faces to the north, and planned the two-hundred-mile journey as best they could. It was a joy to set off on top of the mailcoach, to see the woods and houses snatched back as they flew past, and the weathercocks whirling upon the steeples. Their cheeks glowed with cold; they had to shout to make each other hear above the thunder of the iron-bound wheels and the leaping notes of the coachman's horn.

"All right?" shouted Georg, above the clatter.

"Fine!" shouted Sebastian, swinging his arms across his chest in imitation of the postilion.

Such joys were too fine to last. They had to save their money for occasional coach rides on the highroad. In between they tramped through muddy lanes, stopping to study the milestones or beg a lift in an ox wagon, eating their bread and cheese with numbed fingers under the shelter of a barn. It was near the end of Lent before they began to cross the famous Lüneburg Heath. The pale northern sky, the wide, empty horizon, the endless miles of marsh and heather seemed lonely to these boys from a forest land. Yet they kept on.

"There it is! We are nearly there at last!" shouted Sebastian one morning, and pointed ahead. On the skyline a finger of turquoise blue pointed above a cluster of tiled roofs. It was the copper spire of St. John's Church, the wayfarer's landmark for Lüneburg.

The two boys hurried on as fast as their heavy knapsacks would allow, and found St. Michael's Church, with the old convent where the choirboys lived, just within the city wall. As at Eisenach, the monastic building had become a school during the Reformation.

The buildings around the cloister were of stone; tall, echoing, and dark, they might have daunted any newcomer. But Sebastian was hardy, and settled into the daily life of the school without complaint. The convent bell jangled them awake while it was still dark, and they stumbled out of the dormitory where they all slept in rows upon the floor. Anyone who tried to snatch a few extra minutes on his straw mattress would be kicked and trampled by the others. There was a fight to splash face and hands in the icy water of pump or trough, another fight for the slices of dry, black bread in the refectory. It was a brutal age when little boys, too young to defend themselves at school, were commonly robbed of their food or kicked away from the warmth of the stove. Sebastian's square shoulders and ready fists must have stood him in good stead. He was helped, too, by a tough good humor, a ready fund of puns and jokes, which was to last him a

lifetime. He even made jokes about his name, Bach, which
in German means brook. "He is the only Krebs in my
Bach," he once said of a friend, tickled by the fact that
his name, Krebs, meant "crab." There must have been many
puns on the name of Bach shouted around the choristers'
dormitory.

The boys in the choir school had, by the rules, to be
"the offspring of poor people, with nothing to live on,
but possessing good voices." In return for singing in church
they received board, lodging, firewood and candles, and
a small salary. In Sebastian's time the soprano boys earned
about twelve little silver groschen a month. They also
served and waited on a number of rich young noblemen
who attended the "Knightly Academy" in the same building. Sebastian does not seem to have minded this menial
work; he was used to scrubbing, emptying buckets and
chopping firewood, and he took the opportunity of pick-
ing up French, which the aristocrats used in conversation.
He was proud enough of his French words and phrases
to bring them often into his letters.

The choir of St. Michael's, as elsewhere, made pro-
cessions around the town at Christmas and the New
Year, singing in the cold sleet and slush, until the
masters complained that the boys' voices were ruined.
One hopes that a kindly housewife sometimes took pity
on these charity children, and ran out with bowls of soup
or mulled ale to warm them.

There was a rival choir school at St. John's Church,
which at first attempted to sing in the same streets.

"After them!"

"Chase them off!"

"Thrash them!" yelled the Michaelers, snatching up sticks and stones to charge the enemy. There was a sharp scuffle, and the defeated straggled home with bruised shins and bleeding noses. After that the city council ordered the two schools to make their Currenden on different routes, and so avoid "unseemly wrangles."

The original pre-Reformation choir of St. Michael's had been founded in the thirteenth century, and in 1700, when Sebastian joined it, the music of the church was worthy of its long tradition. The long, dusty shelves of the library held more than a thousand manuscripts of choral music, some as old as the Middle Ages, some by living composers, even some by the great Uncle Christoph of Eisenach. It is not likely that Sebastian was allowed to copy these treasures, at least in his junior years, but he was placed at once in the small choir which sang the most difficult music, and so he must have learned them for perfomance, Sunday by Sunday. His own early compositions show how he had stored them away in his receptive brain.

The services at St. Michael's were long and elaborate. For the main Sunday service, "Hauptgottesdienst," Sebastian put on his black gown and took his place among the sopranos at seven in the morning. The service wound its way through collects, anthems, epistle, gospel, creed, a cantata, a long sermon, sung Holy Communion and further collects. It was midday before the minister uttered the final blessing, and the choirboys could file out to the vestry to blow their numbed fingers alive.

There was just time to go back to the school and gulp their bowls of soup before the afternoon sermon and hymns. It was a strict rule in choir schools that no food was to be taken into the church, but the prefect who seized and shook the little boys for contraband crusts was often glad to swallow them himself in the cloister. Choir rules also allowed the boys to return to the school house and hear a sermon read "if the Inspector declares the cold in church to be beyond their endurance."

Yet Sebastian Bach's whole later life makes it clear that, in spite of cold and hunger, the hours he spent in church were precious to him. The lofty nave of St. Michael's, the clustered pillars, the altarpiece of glowing gold and the music, worthy of this exquisite setting, held all that his life knew of beauty. His strong and simple nature eagerly accepted the stern teaching of the Lutheran Church, that God is our just judge, that man of himself is nothing and can be saved by faith alone.

Still more, this lonely boy, making his own way in the world without a home or the love of parents, opened his heart to the love of God. There was nothing weak or sentimental about Sebastian's faith; into it he poured all the force of his vigorous character and his creative power. He read his Bible constantly and with care, collecting commentaries and religious writings as a hobby, until, when he died, his bookshelves were full of them. His set of Luther's works in eight huge volumes was thumbed and annotated with the reading of a lifetime.

Performing and creating music, in church or out, was always to him a part of God's service. His intense and personal love of the Saviour shines through the notes, as when, in his *St. Matthew Passion*, a string quartet surrounds the words of Jesus with a halo of shimmering sound. From boyhood onwards until almost the day of his death, Sebastian headed each composition with the

letters "J.J." for *"Jesus juva"*—"Jesus help me"—and ended
with "S.D.G." for *"Solo Dei gratia"*—"to God alone the
praise."

Sebastian was already fifteen when he entered St.
Michael's choir, and before many months his beautiful
soprano voice began to play tricks. As he opened his part
book to sing the descant it suddenly leaped down an octave
and sounded strange among the tenors. Then it seemed to
divide, so that for a week he sang and spoke in octaves,
impossible to hide from the Cantor's keen ear.

"Chorister Sebastian Bach, your voice is breaking,"
said the master at once.

"Yes, sir." Sebastian wondered if he would be sent back
to Thuringia, a failure in his first professional engagement.

"You certainly cannot sing," said the Cantor. "You are
now excused from further choir duties."

Sebastian's heart sank.

"However," said the Cantor, "since you are a competent musician, we need not dispense with your services. Attend orchestral rehearsal tomorrow."

Now Sebastian entered on a new stage in his musical
training. The Cantor soon found that his fifteen-year-old
pupil could hold his own with seasoned musicians as a
violinist or viola player, and that he could play the harpsichord brilliantly, either from a figured bass or from
scattered voice parts laid out above the keyboard. From
1700 until 1703, Sebastian earned his living as choir prefect* in charge of the younger boys, orchestral player,

---

*A prefect is a senior boy, trustworthy and responsible, who is
given authority to maintain order and discipline among the
juniors. It is a real honor to hold this position in school, though
it is no longer paid.

and accompanist. When he was given a choice of instrument in the orchestra, his friends always knew what he would choose.

"Let me take the viola part," he used to say. "There I can feel myself in the midst of the harmony, where I can hear it and enjoy it on both sides."

As he was fitting himself for the career of organist and Cantor, Sebastian continued his organ lessons with a great master, Böhm of the St. John's Church.

"Now you are a prefect, and show yourself so trustworthy," Böhm said to him, "they should allow you more freedom. Go to Hamburg and hear old Reinken play on the organ of St. Catherine's. He is one of the greatest organists of our day, and you should hear him."

Sebastian needed no urging. When he was sixteen he got leave of absence during the summer holidays, and set off across the wild and lonely heath to walk the thirty miles to Hamburg. He was hot, dusty, and tired when he arrived, but sitting at Vespers in the great, dim church he felt the music rolling about him like a cool flood as Reinken improvised on the psalm, *By the Waters of Babylon*. He listened and walked away again, unknown and unnoticed, with the splendid melodies still ringing in his head, waiting for the day when they would sound again in his own music.

He had set out on his travels with only a few coppers, which had bought bread and beer in the town. Now it was late afternoon and his stomach began to protest at the long hungry miles on the homeward road. He trudged along, singing to keep up his spirits. An inn sign mocked him with its promise of good cheer, and he sat down on the bench outside, sniffing hungrily at the scent of meat roasting on the kitchen spit. He felt in his pockets—no use, quite empty.

Suddenly a window opened above his head and something was thrown out. Sebastian searched in the wayside grass and found two chopped-off fish heads. He fell on them hungrily, but stopped at the touch of something hard inside. He tore them open and saw a glint of silver. Could it be—two Danish ducats—enough to buy a sumptuous dinner and leave money in hand? Yes, it was true. Some unknown friend had come to the help of the young wanderer.

Sebastian used to chuckle as he told his own sons how he had used some of the money to buy the best dinner at the inn, and the rest to go straight back to Hamburg and hear some more music!

He made several journeys to hear Reinken in the next two years, always on foot; he also walked in the other direction to hear the orchestra at Celle.

Celle was the seat of a Duke, George Wilhelm, who had built an elegant little palace for his French wife in the style of her own country. Its outer walls enclosed a leafy park with statues and fountains; within, it was a miniature French court with candle-lit ballrooms, a private theatre and a tiny chapel, glowing with gold and jewels. Young Sebastian Bach, country bred and solidly German, looked around in wonder at French clothes and manners, and listened fascinated to the elegant French music. There was nothing prim or disapproving about him; in spite of his strict upbringing, he threw himself with delight into the new experience, and was soon copying

French compositions and musical ornament into his own notebooks.

All through these crowded Lüneburg years Sebastian was at work, seizing new impressions, making notes, copying and writing exercises to prepare himself for his own work as a composer. Nothing seemed too big for him to tackle or too small for him to notice. He came to Lüneburg still a boy. When he left in 1703 he was, at eighteen, a man and a musician, with the promise of greatness.

Years later his own pupils would ask him the secret of his amazing skill, and the master always laughed at them.

"There is nothing magical about it," he would say. "When I was young, I had to work hard! Work as hard as I did, and you will do just as well!"

# CHAPTER SIX

# THE YOUNG ORGANIST

## (1703-1707)

At seventeen, Sebastian decided he must find an organ of his own to work on. Other young men, older than himself, stayed on at St. Michael's as choir prefects, sure at least of board and lodging, but he was impatient to master his art.

In July 1702 he applied for the post of organist at Sangerhausen. The town councillors were startled to hear of a boy offering himself so confidently, but on the other hand travelers from Lüneburg all told the same tale, "The playing of young Bach is a wonder!" In the end they elected him organist, but the overlord of the town stepped in.

"A boy of eighteen! Too young—far too young!"

A man eleven years older was appointed and Sebastian found himself without a job. He swallowed his disappointment and in 1703 found work somewhere else. This time it was a humble position as string player in a small band maintained at Weimar by the reigning Duke's younger brother. In the evenings he had to put on bandsmen's livery and fiddle away with the other court servants at his master's amateur compositions. Sebastian was quite cheerful about this, for he had a plan forming in his mind.

Weimar is not far from Arnstadt, and in 1703 the New Church at Arnstadt inaugurated a newly built organ. Following the usual custom, the council invited two experts to examine it. One was "Organist Johann Sebastian Bach" who rode over from Weimar on a hired horse, receiving expenses and a small fee for his trouble. On the Sunday after the inspection, at morning service, the organ was blessed, and Sebastian played publicly to the congregation. The councillors looked at one another in amazement as the splendid chords rolled through their gaunt, bare church. There was a hasty whispering in the vestry.

"Young, yes—but a master of his instrument."

"His very looks show an honest and upright young man."

"Such playing would be the glory of our parish!"

They offered Sebastian the post at once; he accepted and a month later, in August 1703, took up his charge. His duties were set out in a parchment from the council offices. As well as training the choir and playing, he had to be "God-fearing, temperate, well disposed to all folk, eschewing ill company, and in all ways showing yourself an honorable servant and organist before God and your worshipful masters." The council was not going to make any allowance for youthful high spirits.

Once more Sebastian packed his chest and moved to new lodgings. Arnstadt was a lovely hillside town, ringed with old walls and turrets and interlaced with running water. Sebastian's room at the Golden Crown looked onto a crooked square from which the little streets curled away like the finger of a hand. Below his window a fountain plashed unceasingly. By day he saw the cart horses stop

*The Golden Crown at Arnstadt, where Bach stayed*

to drink there, and at night he lay listening to the chuckle of the water as it flowed over the cobblestones.

Now Sebastian had the joy of his new organ—his to play on, without asking permission, whenever he liked. Day after day he worked through his manuscripts, utterly absorbed, while people stopped in the market-place to hear the thunder of the organ notes shaking the windows of the empty church.

Playing the organ and choosing the music for the services gave Sebastian inexhaustible happiness, but there was another side to his duties which he did not enjoy. The organist was saddled with the responsibility of training the unruly, rowdy choristers into a choir worthy of

the music it had to sing. His choirboys were young hooli-
gans from the back streets and alleys of the town, and
the notes of the Arnstadt council relate some of the things
which these particular boys used to do. "They have no
respect for their masters, fight in their presence, come
to school wearing swords, play at ball games in their
classrooms, even in the House of God, and resort to places
of ill repute. Out of school they gamble, drink, and do
other things we shrink from naming. At night they disturb the town with their promenading and shouting."

The gang of louts was an instrument on which Sebastian's musicianship could not play. At first he attempted
to teach them, but when they would not listen, his quick
temper rose at the insult to music. He shouted at them,
turned on his heel, and stalked out of church. Soon he
came to leave them to their own devices and concentrated on his organ practice.

Sebastian was not lonely. Old Great-uncle Heinrich of
Arnstadt had died long ago, and also Uncle Johann Christoph, but there were still a widowed aunt and cousin
living in the cobbled Kohlgasse. Above all there was his
childhood friend, Maria Barbara. She was exactly his age,
and now that her mother had died she was like himself,
alone in the world. As the summer of 1704 ripened into
autumn the two young cousins renewed their old friendship, taking long walks over the hillside and the harvest
fields. To Maria Barbara, Sebastian could tell his vexations.

"That great bully Rambach is called choir prefect, but
all he does for his title is to knock the little boys about.
He is supposed to conduct the choir on Sundays; yet
during the sermon he sneaks out of the organ gallery

and over to the Schwarzburger ale house. When he comes back it is all he can do to conduct his own two legs!"

Maria Barbara listened and nodded her smooth young head. She was Bach enough herself to have no use for idle musicians. Soon she was to see how Sebastian dealt with them.

On a fine spring evening in 1705 he called to take her to the rehearsal of a comic opera he was conducting in Count Anton Günther's private theatre. During the rehearsal a bassoonist fumbled his part and Sebastian spoke sharply to him. Now it was late, and Sebastian was taking her home across the moonlit square. Suddenly there was a shout, and a gang of young men stepped out of the shadow of a long arcade. The leader rushed at them, waving a stick.

"You called me a clumsy fool!" he shouted. "Take that back or be thrashed!"

In an instant Sebastian had placed Maria Barbara safely behind a pillar, whirled round, and drawn his sword.

"You butter-fingered bassoonist!" he said contemptuously. "Out of my way!"

He lunged at his attacker, who set up a roar of alarm. Windows opened and heads popped out, all around the square. Anxious citizens in nightcaps rushed out to separate the opponents, but Sebastian brushed them aside without a word. Casting his cloak around Maria Barbara's shoulders, and tucking her arm under his, he led her home. Next morning found him at work in his organ gallery as usual.

The affair came to the notice of the city council, and during the summer Sebastian was summoned to appear before them. If they expected their young organist to be frightened, they got a surprise. He merely asked for an assistant to train the choir, and for leave of absence himself to go to Lübeck for Advent. From sheer amazement, presumably, the council consented.

So it was that on the second Sunday in Advent, Sebastian sat in the Marienkirche at Lübeck which he had long desired to visit. The great organist, Dietrich Buxtehude was nearly seventy at this time, and towered like a giant above the other musicians of the day.* The climax of the musical year was his "Evening Music," the concerts after Vespers during Advent. Outside it was dark, but within, the great church was packed, and the light of a thousand candles fell upon trumpets, drums, and rows of violins. To Sebastian it was like the courts of heaven; never had he heard music of such scale and splendor. He stayed for another Sunday, and another. During the weeks, he took lessons from the great master, at the organ set so gloriously above the western arch of the Marienkirche. His conception of music grew with a new and disturbing power as his hands flew over the manuals. Sebastian Bach, the artist, was coming of age.

No wonder he lost track of days and weeks. When he returned to Arnstadt, his head full of music, it was January 1706, and he had overstayed his leave by three months.

Maria Barbara listened to all that he had to tell; he

---

*When the time came, Sebastian Bach and G. F. Handel were both considered as his possible successors at the Marienkirche, but both declined on hearing that the new organist would be expected to marry Buxtehude's daughter.

*The organ at Arnstadt on which Sebastian played*

took her hand and led her up into the organ loft, where she sat by his side and heard him improvise with a strength and beauty she had never known before. On the first Sunday after his return the whole congregation could hear him, with surprise and dismay. They found that they could not sing even the simplest hymn tunes when their young organist embroidered upon the melody with such disturbing freedom. They groped for the tune, broke down, and gave up in disgust.

In February, Sebastian was summoned before the consistorium again, and the clerk grimly headed a page in his notebook, "Joh. Seb. Bach, organist of the New Church, summoned to explain his long absence and discontinuance of choral music 1706."

The conversation which followed had its comic side. The superintendent of the council cleared his throat and began impressively:

"The consistorium desires to know where you have been for so long, and who gave you leave of absence."

"I have been to Lübeck to study my profession," answered Sebastian readily, "and before I went, Herr Superintendent, I asked your permission."

"That is so," said the superintendent, "but you said you would be away four weeks and you have been absent four months. Have you any explanation to offer?"

Sebastian could not describe all his tumultuous feelings as he had listened to Buxtehude, and wisely he did not attempt to. The council went on to complain of his new style of playing.

"You accompany the hymns with astounding variations, which throw the congregation into confusion. Furthermore," the superintendent said, becoming more and more exasperated, "you used to play too long preludes, and now I have told you about it, you go to the opposite extreme and make them too short. There is another matter also; you have ceased to perform choral music. If you will not do so, we must find an organist who will."

Sebastian merely bowed and walked out of the room, leaving his employers to shake their heads over the obstinacy of youth. Some would have liked to dismiss him out-of-hand, but others would not.

"No town has an organist as good as this young Bach," they said.

In the end they did nothing.

After this things went more or less smoothly for six

months: Sebastian had plenty to occupy his time. The inspiration of Lübeck was working upon his mind and heart. He had already composed suites for clavichord, but now he began work upon a set of organ preludes and fugues, which foreshadowed his coming greatness.

Maria Barbara shared more and more of his life, and the friendship between them began to blossom with the unfolding summer into first love. Day after day she crept into the church where he was practicing and sat beside him in the organ loft. She was a Bach, a musician as well as a girl in love, and for very joy she could not help singing.

One day a scandalized pastor, coming in suddenly, heard a woman's voice, fresh and clear, ring out from the organ loft. Such a thing was unheard of. Traditionally women took no part in the music of the Lutheran church. He hurried off to the consistorium, and soon the inevitable summons came.

"Organist Johann Sebastian Bach," said the superintendent, "how do you explain the presence of a strange girl in your organ loft?"

Young love, youthful impatience, and family pride combined to make Sebastian revolt. We do not know what answer he made, but in less than a year he had found a new appointment at Mühlhausen, and handed over the key of his Arnstadt organ with a letter of resignation.

# CHAPTER SEVEN

# YOUNG LOVE AND MARRIAGE

## (1707-1708)

In June 1707 Sebastian went to Mühlhausen to settle the terms of his appointment. He was twenty-two and wished to marry, so he made himself what he always remained, a good business man. His terms to his new parish of St. Blaise were quite clear: "85 gulden in money, 3 measures of corn, 2 trusses of wood—one of beech, one of oak— and 6 trusses of faggots delivered at his door." He also held out for a wagon to bring his clavier and small stock of furniture from Arnstadt. The council agreed and the bargain was sealed by a simple shaking of hands, which Sebastian honored as faithfully as an oath.

By September he had settled in, and something else happened to forward his plans. An uncle, whom he hardly knew, died, and left him fifty gulden. Next month he was back in Arnstadt for his wedding with Maria Barbara. The harvest was in, and the stubble fields were golden in the sunshine as he walked up the steep path to the village of Dornheim. There in the little white-walled church he exchanged rings with his cousin and received the blessing of the pastor, who was a friend of the family. Their entry still stands in the register:

"On Oct. 17th 1707 the worthy Joh. Seb. Bach, bachelor, organist of the church of Divi Blasii Mühlhausen, son of the deceased honorable and distinguished Ambrosius Bach, musician of Eisenach, to the virtuous Maria Barbara, daughter of the right worthy and distinguished Michael Bach, organist at Gehren, here in this House of God."

Sebastian and Maria Barbara, being both orphans, were too poor for the full ceremonial of a Thuringian marriage, when an ox or sheep was usually roasted whole, but the bride, however poor, followed the custom and baked the loaves with her own hands. On her wedding day she wore a wreath of fresh myrtle upon glossy braids of hair, and the young men brought the bridegroom to church with songs and trumpets. The rafters of Dornheim church can never have rung with the singing of so many good musicians as at the wedding of two Bachs.

The young husband and wife had neither time nor money for a long honeymoon, and within a week they were back at Mühlhausen for Sebastian to play at the Sunday services. They had to lodge in a distant suburb, because a disastrous fire in May of that year had destroyed almost the whole center of the town. Yet as he walked back through the blackened streets, past rows of ruined houses, Sebastian knew that for the first time since childhood he was returning to a real home. Maria Barbara's hands had polished their few possessions with loving care, she had set the pewter dishes on the table for his homecoming, and now she waited to welcome him beside their own hearth.

Family happiness and high resolve swept Sebastian

onwards in his career. He loved the beauty of his new church, its twin towers, soaring arches, and rose window, but found the organ in bad repair.

He asked permission to test it and set to work with his usual thoroughness. He tested each part in turn and wrote a most workmanlike specification, which the council carried out with great good will. On this improved organ he played every Sunday and for holy days.

Now that he was a married man and a "Master Musician," his wandering years of training over, Sebastian followed the usual German custom and took a pupil into the house. Martin Schubarth, who came to live with his master, was only five years younger than Sebastian and Maria Barbara, and became their devoted friend. For ten years he shared their house, moved with them, played with their children, and helped to copy Sebastian's music. When he left to become an organist, another pupil followed him, and another, right to the end of Sebastian's life.

These young musicians stayed for years in the house, and twenty years later sent their own sons in turn to be pupils of the great Bach.

When they went out into the world as organists and choir masters they remembered the hours thay had spent in his house as the happiest in their lives. One said, long afterwards, that he could never forget the times when Sebastian did not feel like teaching and sat down at the clavier to play. Then, wrote the pupil, "the hours seemed to be but minutes." Another, Christian Kittel, used to keep Sebastian's portrait hanging above the organ, as in a shrine. A third, Philipp Kirnberger, kept a portrait in his room to look at every day. A visitor made fun of it.

"Good Lord, you have old Bach there, hanging on the wall! The vain fool has had himself painted in a splendid velvet coat!"

Kirnberger rushed at his guest, seized him by the collar, and ran him out of the room, shouting "Out, dog! Out, dog!"

Such was the love and reverence of Sebastian's pupils for their master.

On his side, as he grew older, he came to have a father's feelings for them. The testimonials he wrote to recommend them for jobs were not a formality, but show a feeling all the deeper for being restrained.

"I therefore trust he will obtain God's assistance to help him to advancement, and I recommend him once again with all my heart."

Teaching, practicing, and organ-building were not enough to exhaust Sebastian's energies during his stay at Mühlhausen. Now his true creative powers began to show themselves, and he threw himself into composition.

For the inauguration of a new Burgomaster he wrote a cantata, *God is my King*, which was performed with splendid ceremony in the Marienkirche. He took endless pains with the score, which can still be seen, corrected and re-corrected in his vigorous handwriting. Sudden scratches and blots show where the quill feather could not keep pace with his flying thoughts, and sharp crossing out shows where he impatiently dismissed the second-best.

It was a proud day for Maria Barbara when she saw her husband conducting singers, trumpets, strings, and drums in the western gallery and heard the splendor of his music rolling through the nave. The Mühlhausen council was so impressed by the cantata that it was printed at the city's expense, the only cantata by Sebastian to see print in his lifetime.

May, 1708 was the anniversary of the great fire, and Sebastian composed a cantata on the poignant text, "Out of the deep have I cried to Thee: Lord, hear my voice." June brought a happier task—the composing of a wedding cantata for the pastor friend who had performed the marriage service for the Bachs at Dornheim, and who was now marrying in his turn. Sebastian's life was slipping into the rhythm it was to hold to its end—a rhythm of creation as constant as the beating of his heart.

The work of composition did not go forward at Mühlhausen without difficulties. Sebastian's music was valued in the city and the surrounding countryside, and by Dr. Eilmar, the minister of the Marienkirche. Matters stood very differently at his own church of St. Blaise. The minister of St. Blaise, Pastor Frohne, belonged to the group within the Lutheran church known as the Pietists. For him, religion was not creeds and church services, but prayer, Bible study, and piety in everyday life. So far Sebastian, who was, with all his genius, a simple and faithful man, agreed with him. Unfortunately the good pastor like all Pietists, also denounced dancing, the theatre, the most harmless games, and all music as snares of the devil, thundering from the pulpit against Sebastian's musical friend, Dr. Eilmar.

Sebastian was quite clear in his own mind about the place of music in worship, and about the purpose of music generally. "All music," he cried, "should have no other end and aim than the glory of God and the soul's refreshment; where this is not remembered there is no true music."

Since he and his pastor could not agree on this cardinal point, Sebastian judged that he would do better to find another appointment, where he could work without opposition. In June 1708 he accepted an invitation to the court of Weimar, and resigned from Mühlhausen. The letter in which he gave his reasons to the city council was remarkable for a young man of twenty-three.

"... It has been my constant aim that church music should be so performed as to exalt God's glory, and, as far as my humble ability has allowed, I have assisted that purpose also in the neighboring villages. But I have not been allowed to do my work without opposition, and there does not seem to be the least *apparence* that it will abate, though in time perhaps some of our church's congregation may be brought to approve. Moreover, if I may say so respectfully, frugal as is my household, I have not enough to live on.

God has been pleased, however, to open to me an unexpected situation, and better subsistence, and, what concerns me most, an opportunity to pursue the betterment of church music, free from the opposition and vexations encountered here. His Serene Highness the Duke of Saxe-Weimar has been pleased to give me the *entrée* to his Capelle. I convey this information to you, with profound respect, begging your generous permission to retire...."

There was nothing to be done in face of a letter so courteous yet so frank and firm. The Mühlhausen council accepted Sebastian's resignation and in July 1708 the Bach household packed up once more and took the road to Weimar.

Sebastian never moved far from his birthplace. In all his life he never saw the sea, or heard people converse in a language that was not his native German. Most of his journeys were not more than a day's travel from one small walled city to another. Yet the strongest natures cannot be bound by time and space, and within the narrow circle he kept his spirit free.

CHAPTER EIGHT

## COURT-ORGANIST AT WEIMAR

### (1708-1717)

Germany, in Sebastian's lifetime, was divided into many dukedoms and principalities, some smaller than an English county, yet each ruled by its own "Serene Highness."

Weimar took its character from Duke Wilhelm. The town was sober as he was sober, pious as he was pious, thrifty and industrious under his keen eye. The stiff ceremonial of the little court revolved around him; the burghers put out garlands of green leaves in his honor as he passed through the town; the peasants by the roadside bowed or curtsied as his coach thundered past.

The old houses of the town were still enclosed by their medieval wall, and a visitor who wished to pass in or out had to sign his name in the Guard House at one of the four gates. On Sundays a chain held back the crowd as the Duke walked in solemn procession across the square to church, where he decided the order in which his servants should approach the Communion table.

Duke Wilhelm was determined that his servants should lead a Christian life and he was not a man one could disobey. Plays and actors were forbidden, the castle bearpit was turned into a flower garden, and the last light was blown out at eight o'clock in winter and at nine in summer. Sober clergy paced through the courts and ballrooms of the palace. The ruler himself, in his moated castle, brooded over the life of court and town.

"Listen carefully to the sermon!" Sebastian was warned. "You can be sure he'll question you about every word the chaplain says. Then you must be punctual for court prayers every morning, and look on the list to see when it's your turn to read the lesson. It's all religion here!"

Whatever their fellow musicians thought, the solemnity of life in Weimar did not trouble Sebastian and Barbara. The parents of a young family cannot go out much at the best of times, and their home soon began to fill with children. The first was born at Christmas 1708—a little girl, Catharina, who was the joy of her mother, and who would one day be the comfort of her father's old age. Three little boys followed, among them Wilhelm Friedemann and Carl Phillip Emmanuel, the most gifted of Sebastian's sons, of whose training we shall hear later. Twins were born, but soon died, and were buried by their young parents with sorrow, but without complaint. Like all their generation, they had been brought up on the stern text, "The Lord hath given and the Lord hath taken away."

Maria Barbara was quite lost from view in the cares of her household. After the first glimpses of her in the organ gallery and the winding streets of Arnstadt, she disappears from the written records of Sebastian's life and it is only from pictures of the period that we can imagine her working by his side. In brown woolen gown, with cap and apron of starched linen, she treads the family washing in the brook, scours the tiled floor, or carries the wooden bucket to the fountain in the square. On summer evenings she spins in the courtyard of the little house, her ear alert for a cry from the cradle, or listening with contentment to the sound of the clavier from Sebastian's music room.

On some evenings Sebastian's friends come to share the pleasure of music or good talk. One was Salomo Franck, the Duke's librarian and keeper of his collection of coins, a deeply read and thoughtful man, in whose company Sebastian delighted. By happy chance Franck was also a poet, who wrote the words of cantatas for Sebastian to compose, and gave him during the years at Weimar some of the finest texts he ever had to work on.

Another member of the circle was a young scholar, Matthias Gesner, who at twenty-four already had a profound knowledge of Greek and Latin literature. Scholar and musician felt an instinctive sympathy for each other. Years later they were to meet again as colleagues in Leipzig, when Gesner showed his deep admiration for Sebastian's genius.

Another friend was Johann Gottfried Walther, organist of the Town Church, who could give Sebastian the stimulating companionship of a fellow-professional. They exchanged musical greetings in canon form, and once Walther played a musical joke on his friend.

Sebastian, usually so modest, was rash enough to say that he could read any piece of music at sight. Walther skilfully arranged a piece of music full of traps and pitfalls, which he left open on the clavier when Sebastian was due to call.

Sebastian arrived and looked around: no Walther, but new music on the stand. He could never resist new music.

He sat down to play—and stumbled at one passage. He looked at it and began again, only to blunder at the same place. His quick temper rose. "No!" he cried, "No, it's impossible! It can't be done!" Suddenly he heard his friend shouting with laughter in the next room. Walther came in, still laughing, and clapped him affectionately on the shoulder.

"I take it back," said Sebastian. "The man doesn't live who can play *everything* at sight."

One feels the family happiness behind the flowering of Sebastian's genius in these years, from twenty-three to thirty-two, which he spent at Weimar. It is above all the time of his greatness as organist, student of organ building, and composer for the organ—the greatest in the history of music.

He went every day to practice in the castle, across the drawbridge and into the many-colored Baroque chapel, where sculptured cupids climbed a marble pyramid called "The Way to the Heavenly City." It was a strange setting for the austere and noble music he created.

Stories began to go around about the miraculous skill of the young organist at Weimar: for instance, that he had visited a village church where he was unknown, and had played so that the pastor whispered, "It is Bach or the devil himself!" Yet technical skill at the expense of the music itself did not interest Sebastian, and he used to reply with dry humor to people who lavishly praised his playing, "There is nothing in it. All you do is hit the right notes at the right time and the organ plays itself."

Duke Wilhelm was not slow to see what glory this

fine performer shed on his court, and used to take his organist with him upon state visits. Sebastian's thick-set figure must have looked strange in the court livery which was made like a hussar's costume, with bearskin, military tunic, and high boots. But in the simplicity of his greatness he recognized that he had to earn bread for his family, and accepted the conditions of service without complaint.

Perhaps he enjoyed his visits to other courts. At Cassel "his feet flying over the pedals as though they were winged, made the notes reverberate like thunder in a storm," and the Prince pulled a ring from his finger to present to the player. At Weissenfels in 1716, for the wedding of the Duke's young brother, the guests sat down to a banquet in a vast hall where tubs of cypress, orange, almond, and myrtle made summer in the midst of winter. At the wedding Sebastian produced a cantata containing one of his best-loved airs, *Sheep may safely graze.*

Among his fellow musicians Sebastian was specially valued as an authority on the building and repair of organs, and all through his life he made journeys by invitation to examine various instruments. He always began by drawing out all the stops to hear the Full Organ sound. "Let us find out if it has good lungs," he used to say. His sons remembered that towards organs, as towards men, he was "very severe but always just. It was impossible to deceive him, and his opinion carried great weight among his colleagues."

When he had finished his testing of the fine new organ of the Liebfrauenkirche at Halle in 1716 a banquet was given in his honor, of which the menu is preserved.

Boeuf à la mode.
Pike with anchovy butter.
Smoked Ham.
Peas and Potatoes.
Sausages and Spinach.
A quarter of Roast Mutton.
Boiled Pumpkin.
Fritters.
Candied Lemon Peel and Cherries.
Asparagus, Lettuces, Radishes.
Fresh Butter.
Roast Veal.

It must have been a change from the thrifty simplicity of Barbara's housekeeping!

Handel was born at Halle, and had his first organ lessons as a boy in the Liebfrauenkirche. Sebastian greatly wished to meet him, but Handel rarely left England and their paths never crossed.

In 1717 Sebastian Bach's fame was to spread throughout Germany. A famous French organist, Louis Marchand, visited Dresden, and Sebastian, always eager to hear fine playing, went there to listen to him. Two masters of the organ in the town at once! The news spread through Dresden society and gossips in ballrooms or coffee houses could talk of nothing else.

"Have you heard the latest? Count von Flemming has persuaded Bach to challenge the Frenchman to a public trial of skill! They will both play the clavier in his music room and all Dresden will be there to judge between them!"

The day came, and the company assembled. Sebastian was impatient, but was, nevertheless, punctual and civil. They waited while the gilt clock ticked through a quarter, a half, a whole hour. A footman was sent to Marchand's lodgings and returned.

"The Frenchman has fled!"

Marchand had listened secretly to Sebastian practicing, and dared not face the unequal contest. He had left Dresden in the early morning to avoid public humiliation.

It was the first time a German organist had been unquestioned master, and the news of Sebastian's triumph spread through all the little courts of Germany.

For us today, Bach the performer and organ-builder is lost, but as a composer for the organ he is as inexhaustible as the stars or the sky itself. In his twenties he had already composed in his own highly personal style. The old German tradition in which he had been bred, the French and Italian styles he had studied, were fused by his great heart and brain into something new and unmistakable —the music of Bach.

At Weimar he wrote a number of *Arrangements of Violin Concertos* by Italian masters for clavier and organ. He followed these by a series of splendid *Preludes and Fugues, Three Toccatas and Fugues*, the *Fantasias* and the great *Passacaglia in C minor*—touchstone of all organists. However severe or limiting the form he chose, its difficultes seemed to inspire him to creation.

At the same time he began the series of *Church Cantatas* which he was to continue for the rest of his life. Already he pondered the meaning of his texts, and taught his pupils "when playing hymns not to treat the melody as if it alone were important, but to interpret the words through the melody."

Another group of organ works from the Weimar years are the *Chorale Preludes*. These were the passages of free improvisation with which the organist surrounded the hymn tunes in church. Sebastian probably wrote down only a few of those he actually played, and most of these we owe to a misfortune which overtook him in 1717.

In December 1716, Duke Wilhelm's old court Kapell-meister, or Master of Music, had died. The old man had long been incapable of doing all his work and much of it had been carried by Sebastian, who naturally expected to succeed him. He was disappointed when the old man's son, an inferior musician, was appointed over his head. It was not the Bach way to lie down under a slight, and since there was now no hope of promotion at Weimar, Sebastian prepared to look for another appointment.

Duke Wilhelm had a young nephew, friendly and musical, who wanted to help the court organist. He introduced Sebastian to a relative, Prince Leopold of Anhalt-Cöthen, a deep and perceptive lover of music. Nothing would please Prince Leopold better than to have the famous Bach at his court, and he offered Sebastian an appointment as Kapellmeister. Sebastian accepted gladly, and applied for his release from Weimar.

Duke Wilhelm was furious. He disliked his nephew, and did not want to lose his best musician.

"Permission is refused," he said.

He had reckoned without Sebastian Bach. Soon the court chamberlain returned, pale and worried.

"Court organist Bach persists in obstinately demanding his instant release," he said in a faltering voice.

The Duke's dark and heavy features drew together in a scowl.

"Send him to me!"

No one knows what passed between them, or if Sebastian's celebrated temper got the better of him again. But at the end of the interview he was under arrest, and the soldiers marched him off to prison in the Guard House.

There he stayed for nearly a month, from November 6th to December 2nd, 1717. Imprisonment could not move him once his mind was made up. He was not even unhappy. Probably Barbara could bring him baskets of food and clean clothes, and take the children to walk in the street below and wave to him in his window. He could watch the old roofs of the town and the rooks flying homeward at evening.

Above all he had music. It rang clearly in his head, without need of strings or keyboard. He always composed in his head, and did not need to try his themes over on an instrument. Indeed, he had great contempt for musicians who composed at the clavier, and called them "cavaliers of the keyboard." In this month he planned and composed one of his most precious works, *The Little Organ Book*, containing forty-six choral preludes based on hymn tunes.

One could hardly guess at the loveliness of the book's contents from the modest title he gave it. "A little Book for the Organ, wherein the beginner may learn to perform Chorals of every kind, and also acquire skill in the Use of the Pedal.

To God alone the praise be given
For what herein's to man's use written."

The *Orgelbüchlein* is inexhaustible, like a fountain or a spring in the forest, as fresh and clear now as on the day Bach closed its pages. He did not have time to complete the scheme he had planned, for early in December Duke Wilhelm gave way with a bad grace and released him "with notice of his unfavorable dismissal." By Christmas the whole Bach family was in a new home at Cöthen.

# CHAPTER NINE

## KAPELLMEISTER AT CÖTHEN

### (1717-1720)

The five years which Sebastian spent in the service of
Prince Leopold at Cöthen form a sort of idyll in his
life. For a time he pushed his boat out of the main stream
of church music, and lingered, as long as it pleased him,
in the leafy backwater of this little court. Cöthen was a
long summer's day in the middle of a life which had its
share of bleak winds and winter weather.

Anhalt-Cöthen was small, even among the states of
Germany, so small that a man on horseback could ride
across it in one day. The capital, at Cöthen, was a handful
of winding streets and whitewashed houses. There are
varying opinions about the house in which Bach lived,
but he was regarded as one of the senior court officials
and probably lived in the castle as they did. It was sep-
arated from the town by a wooded park. The buildings
stood on three sides of a quadrangle and looked, on the
fourth side, over a prospect of terraced gardens. Three
towers rose clear above the treetops, and on a bright day
one could see for miles, across the roofs of the town and
the sandy plain interlaced with rivers, to the distant hills
and pine forests. The castle was surrounded by a moat

where swans drifted upon the reedy water. So they floated
on many an evening while Sebastian's music was borne
across the water from the candle-lit hall above.

In Prince Leopold, Sebastian found the ideal patron.

"How happy I am to find a prince who not only loves
but understands music," he said.

The Prince was nine years younger than his chief
musician, and romantic in temperament. Instead of a formal wig, he wore his own hair, long and waving; in his
portrait his large clear eyes shine with intelligence. Above
all he was passionately musical. He could play the violin,
viola de gamba and clavier, and sing in a pleasant voice.
From the first he treated Sebastian, not as master to
servant, but with real affection as a fellow musician and
a friend. After the stifling etiquette of Duke Wilhelm's
court it was a most refreshing change.

The salary Sebastian received was four hundred thalers
a year, a useful income for a man with a growing family;
and he valued it for experience had taught him to be a
realist in money matters. Moreover he now found himself
in complete control of an orchestra of eighteen excellent
musicians, with whom he rehearsed regularly in his own
rooms.

Sebastian, with his quick temper and his unfailing
standard of perfection, was a formidable conductor. Musicians who had played under him never forgot it. "He
heard the slightest wrong note, even in the largest cam-
bination," said one, ruefully, years later. Nevertheless, he
knew how to get the best from an orchestra, and now
he had one worthy of his music.

There was no opportunity for composing church music

in Cöthen, since the Prince belonged to the Reformed Church, a branch of the Protestant Church in Germany which followed the teaching of Calvin, the Swiss reformer, with very austere doctrine and an extremely simple form of worship which allowed only plain psalm-singing in its services. What Prince Leopold wanted was music for pleasure. Sebastian's genius adapted itself, apparently without strain, to different work, and for the next six years he produced the enchanting chamber music by which the modern concert-goer chiefly knows him.

It is pleasant to imagine the "Music Evenings" in Prince Leopold's castle. The candles are lit in the great hall, and their flames reflect like stars in the long wall mirrors. A velvet chair is set upon a dais for the young Prince. He appears, bowing graciously to right and left, and the ladies and gentlemen of the court subside, with a rustle of silks, upon narrow gilt benches. There is a polite buzz of conversation. Then—

"Hush, here comes the band!"

Sebastian leads his musicians in and bows to the Prince. He has traveled far from the penniless orphan boy of Eisenach. Now, in his thirties, he is a man of substance, tranquil and assured, his shoulders already bowed from stooping over the keyboard. He wears a coat of dark velvet adorned with rows of gold buttons, a finely pleated shirt of lawn, and the curling white wig of a courtier.* His mouth keeps its firm set, and his eyes their old steadiness. Only a few crowsfeet and a habitual half-frown betray the

---

*A portrait of him in court-dress, painted in 1723, is now in a private collection in the United States.

*Johann Sebastian Bach in court dress, with one of his organs in the background*

strain on his eyes of hours of music-copying. Such a man is Kapellmeister Bach.

The players range themselves around him at the clavier. They too wear court livery and powdered wigs, and their excellent musical instruments shine with much polishing. The Kapellmeister taps his music stand for attention, and the music begins.

What music they heard upon those evenings! The lovely *Brandenburg Concertos* rang out under the painted ceiling, and the four *Suites* danced their own way though the Prince's ballroom. The orchestral players at Cöthen were all good enough musicians to play the solo parts in the *Concertos* for one or more violins, for flute, oboe, and trumpet. Probably the Prince himself took his place as soloist in the *Sonatas* for viola da gamba and clavier. Later the room was hushed as Sebastian, at the clavier, played his own exquisite *Fantasias*, and the *French Suites*, at once so gay and so tender.

Sebastian worked continuously during these Cöthen years, and at high speed, so that we can hardly follow the range of his thought. Yet in his music there is no sign of strain or effort. It is as natural and fresh as flowers in spring.

There was happiness in Sebastian's home now—laughter and the chatter of young voices around his dining table. During these years he had the joy of seeing his children growing up in an atmosphere of good will. In 1718, when the last of his children by Maria Barbara was born, the Prince himself offered to stand godfather, and the baby received the aristocratic names of Leopold Augustus.

The oldest girl, Catharina, could lead her brothers by

the hand, or Barbara could carry the baby across the drawbridge to the old tilting ground where the Prince's cavalry horses exercised each morning. There they played hopscotch or singing games, and stopped to watch in wonder as the splendid sleek horses went thundering by. There, too, Sebastian could stroll on summer evenings, smelling the scent of lime blossoms from the avenue, or leading his boys for walks into the countryside.

As first Friedemann and then Emmanuel reached the age of nine, Sebastian, following the family tradition, began to teach them music himself. The two little boys were very unlike in looks and temperament. Carl Phillip Emmanuel took after his father, with the heavy features, square shoulders, and determination of a true Bach. Friedemann, the older, had rare good looks, a haunting smile, and a long, elegant hand which belied his half-peasant origins. However unlike in looks, they were both gifted, intelligent boys and one can easily imagine the happiness their father found in teaching them. "They are all born musicans," he wrote to a friend.

Sebastian did not regard it as a waste of time for an important composer to spend his mornings teaching small boys. The planning of a course of instruction satisfied his keen and logical mind, and his teaching was, above all, creative. The notebook in which Sebastian set down Friedemann's lessons shows how he taught. First came the prayer, *In Nomine Jesu,* then the clefs, the fingering, the exercises, and a series of carefully graded pieces. During these early lessons with Friedemann, Sebastian created exquisite miniatures which pianists still cherish: *The Little*

*Clavier Book for W. F. Bach, The Little Preludes for Beginners,* and the *Two and Three Part Inventions.*

Carl Phillip Emmanuel remembered the creation of these pieces, and wrote:

"If he found that anyone, after months of practice, began to lose patience, he was kind and wrote little connecting pieces, in which the exercises were linked together. He wrote them down during the hours of teaching, for the immediate need of the pupil; afterwards he transformed these pieces into beautiful and expressive little works of art."

To listen to them now is to see morning sunlight in the music room, the little boy sitting straight and proud at the clavier, and the teacher of genius by his side.

Sometimes the music lessons had to be interrupted when Sebastian's duties took him away from home. Prince Leopold could not bear to be parted from his musicians, above all from his dear Kapellmeister Bach, and used to take them in his suite when he went traveling. State visits to the stiff little courts of Germany were wearisome, but Sebastian could always turn from the boredom of levees and receptions to the inward joys of composing. In 1721, traveling in Prince Leopold's service, he used a prolonged visit to plan and compose twenty-four Preludes and Fugues which form the first book of the *Well-tempered Clavier.*

He headed the manuscript with one of his usual modest and sensible titles, "Composed and put forth for the

*The little boy sat straight and proud at the clavier, the teacher of genius by his side*

Use and Profit of young Musicians anxious to learn, and as a Pastime for others, already expert in the Art." In fact the Preludes and Fugues, one for each major and minor key, were a daring experiment in the possibilities of a new system of tuning the clavier.* They are utterly satisfying to mind and heart, for no two are alike, and each one is a world in itself, grave or gay. Robert Schumann said the last word about the *Well-tempered Clavier.* "It should be every musician's daily bread."

To hear this music, so serene and collected, one could never imagine that the composer of them had just suffered a bitter grief. Yet in 1720, only a year before, disaster had ruined the Bachs' idyllic life. First the baby, the Prince's godson, had died, before they could light one candle on his carved wooden birthday ring. The parents comforted each other, and in the spring Sebastian left with the Prince, who was going to take the cure at Carlsbad.

There for three months the orchestra played each day, while Leopold drank the salty spa water and paced up and down among the pine trees. No news came from home, but letters then were luxuries for the rich and not often to be expected by a mere musician. The visit dragged

---

*For the benefit of piano students, this "equal temperament" is the method we now use, in which all the semitones are of equal size. Sebastian was quick to see that with this system any note could serve as the tonic, since sharps and flats would never sound "out of tune." He demonstrated this by composing in each key in turn.

Incidentally, he always tuned his own claviers, with amazing speed and accuracy.

on, and it was July before the homeward party saw the towers of Cöthen castle rise above the trees.

The Bach children were not playing on the tilting ground, nor were they waiting by the bridge to meet their father. Sebastian rode on. There was no smoke from his chimney, no pot of fresh herbs upon his kitchen window sill, no sign of life in his home.

We do not know how he learned the news. Perhaps the twelve-year-old Catharina ran out to him, with little Bernhard clinging to her skirts. Perhaps some kind neighbor, who had taken the children in, was waiting with an explanation: the heat of summer, a sudden sickness, no time to send a message .... Maria Barbara was dead, and the record can still be seen, as he read it on the page of the parish register.

"On July 7th, 1720 Maria Barbara, wife of Hr. J. S. Bach, Kapellmeister to His Highness and Prince, was buried."

This was the end of the gaiety and laughter at Cöthen. The four children were motherless and Sebastian had lost the faithful companion of thirteen years.

His grief was great, but he found strength to bear it. Death to him was but the casting off of the body, and the release of the soul. It had never been far from his thoughts, and as he grew older he came to await it for himself with a serene longing that shines through all his music.

In the sorrow of Barbara's loss he began to feel something lacking in the life of Cöthen, with all its pleasures. How could he express his innermost faith except through church music? He turned to the pages of his Luther, and found the dedication to the hymns: "Let the Word of God dwell among our people by means of song."

From 1720 onwards Sebastian began to seek for a place as church musician.

# CHAPTER TEN

# ANNA MAGDALENA

## (1720-1723)

Sebastian's first attempt to find a church appointment took him to Hamburg in the winter of 1720, to compete with other musicians for the organ of the Jacobikirche. He was deeply moved to see that one of his judges was an old man, paper-thin and frail. It was Reinken, for whose playing he had walked to Hamburg nearly twenty years before, when he was a choirboy at Lüneburg. Old thoughts, old feelings overwhelmed him and he could only express them by choosing for his improvisation the chorale, *By the Waters of Babylon,* which Reinken had played on that evening long ago.

The old organist listened as Sebastian played variation after variation, piling up arches and pinnacles of glorious sound upon the familiar melody.

"I thought this art was dead, Master Bach," he said, "but I see it still lives in you."

It was the perfect meeting of old master and young. However, Sebastian was not destined to stay in Hamburg. The city council asked him to pay for his appointment with a money present, and this he proudly refused to do. A Bach must have no slur upon his skill or honesty. Se-

bastian clapped on his three-cornered hat and rode home
to his motherless family.

It was the custom in the Bach family, and in German
society generally, for a widower to remarry at once, as
Sebastian's father had done. Yet it was not in his nature
to let old ties slip easily, and for a year and a half he
struggled to look after his children himself.

It was December 1721 before a small group of rel-
atives and close friends gathered in Sebastian's lodgings
for his marriage, by the Prince's special license, to Anna
Magdalena Wülckens. The bridegroom was a man of
thirty-six, the bride a girl of twenty. Sebastian was now
thoughtfully mature. Magdalena, as we picture her from
a little poem he wrote, shines with the radiance of youth.

> "My sweet girl-bride, your servant I,
> Much joy in this day's feast!
> With little flowered galaxy,
> Beauty for bridal dressed.
> So much my heart laughs and resounds
> With pleasure at your being,
> That my deep feeling breaks its bounds,
> My soul in music freeing."

The poem tells us how deeply Sebastian was in love,
and indeed theirs was a love match on both sides.

Anna Magdalena, like Sebastian, was a musician and
the child of musicians. She had come to Cöthen with
her father, who held the post of court trumpeter there;
and as her lovely soprano voice developed and was
trained, she stepped into the position of court singer. So

it was that Sebastian met her, in the course of their work as members of the Prince's Kapelle.

One can imagine them both in Prince Leopold's music room, the Kapellmeister delicately touching the clavier to accompany the young singer by his side. Her dress of stiff brocade is cut low to reveal her shoulders, and the jewels in her hair tremble lightly, as she winds her way through some elaborate Italian aria. Sebastian had a portrait of his young wife painted and this in itself was a very unusual distinction for people of their class. The picture has been lost, apparently forever. All we can say is that to him she was beautiful.

About her character we know a good deal more. Her youth made her naturally Sebastian's pupil and she learned from him with eager intelligence. The year after their marriage he made her a *Clavier-book for Anna Magdalena Bach,* and three years later a larger book, with her initials stamped in gold on the green cover. Inside is a miscellany of music copied or composed for her, rules for playing a figured bass, and a note which promised to teach her the rest by word of mouth. The musician had only the bass part in notes. The upper parts were indicated by figures, which had to be translated at sight into musical intervals—a feat demanding considerable skill. A song reveals their continuing love, and shows how naturally Sebastian mingles the thoughts of love and death.

"If thou art near I go with joy,
To death and to my rest,
If I might know thy loving hand
My closing eyelids pressed."

In addition to teaching Magdalena to play the clavier and to read figured bass, Sebastian taught her to write music, and for the rest of her life she helped him in the endless task of music-copying. She came to write an excellent music hand, which experts can hardly distinguish from her master's.

As Sebastian grew older, his natural obstinacy and hot temper hardened, until every disappointment in his professional work created a crisis in their lives. Through it all, Magdalena stood by him with complete loyalty, not only because she loved him as a husband, but because she revered his creative work. When they were first married she kept her position as court singer, and her earnings made up a third of their family income, but when the time came to give up her career for the sake of Sebastian's, she willingly renounced it forever.

Anna Magdalena did not marry Sebastian alone. At the age of twenty she had to take charge of his four children, his pupils, his guests, and a busy, complicated household. Catharina was only seven years younger than herself, and the two worked side by side through the years, until Sebastian's death, apparently in complete love and friendship. Friedemann was more difficult. A handsome, gifted boy and his father's favorite, he was eleven when his mother died, and perhaps he was jealous of the charming young stepmother who came to take her place. As he grew older there was something restless and moody about him and he did not have the steadiness of the Bachs, which Emmanuel so fully inherited. As the two younger boys were growing up, Anna Magdelena had the joys and sorrows of her own motherhood to bear. In all, thirteen babies were born to her, and we shall see what became of them.

As the mistress of this large household Anna Magdalena was a triumphant success. She kept open house to a never-ending stream of relations, pupils, friends, and visiting musicians, and people always felt happy under her roof. With all her domestic responsibilities she never lost that heightened joy in small things which belongs to the artist. We catch charming glimpses of her in the letters of a nephew who lived in the house and acted as secretary to Sebastian.

Our lovable "Frau Mama" has been ill, but longs to accept an invitation to visit her girlhood home. When the family receives a gift of venison, she roasts it and they all eat it "with great delight." Sebastian tells her of a tame linnet he had heard in his travels which has been taught to sing beautiful songs. She loves song birds so much that he tries to buy it for her. Someone has given her, in her town dwelling, a present of six carnation plants, and she "treasures them as highly as children do their Christmas presents, and tends them with all the care given to babies, lest a single one wither."

It is impossible to read about Anna Magdalena Bach without loving her. Certainly Sebastian's good angel was standing by him at his second wedding.

A week after the sober little ceremony in Sebastian's study, another much larger wedding took place in the castle chapel. Prince Leopold led his cousin Henrietta of Anhalt to the altar, and for five weeks the court was turned upside down by wedding festivities. The bridegroom rushed hither and thither, supervised the decoration

of his wife's boudoir, directed a military parade by his
guards, and sent out invitations to a court ball. The little
bride, elegant and feather-brained, sailed through the
figures of the dance in her richly jeweled ball dress, but
found time to cast an unfriendly eye on her husband's
Kapellmeister. She had heard too much of "dear Bach"
and the happy, quiet hours in the music room. Her own
taste was for livelier pleasures, and she intended that
Leopold should share them. As the court returned to nor-
mal after the wedding festivities, her jealousy of Sebastian
became plain. At concerts she yawned openly, and her
boredom distracted Leopold, who in turn became uneasy.

"She is an *amusa*," said Sebastian, "that is to say a
person without love for the muses. Alas, we shall soon
see his musical ardor abating."

Sebastian was a shrewd judge. Leopold had less and
less time to give to music. Without it, the life of the little
court was empty and unsatisfying.

"It is time to make a change," said Sebastian to Magdalena, after they had been married six months. "Here I
can neither create, nor praise God in music. Besides, I
intend my sons to be university scholars. Heaven alone
knows what the lack of a university education meant
to me."

"You are yourself, my dearest," she answered. "What
university could make you greater than you are?"

Nevertheless when the cantor of St. Thomas's Church
and School at Leipzig died in 1722, she encouraged him
to apply for the post. At first Sebastian refused. He was
a man of his times, sensitive to social rank, and it was a
step down from Kapellmeister to mere Cantor. He settled

down to the revision of his *Well-tempered Clavier,* to
teaching the children, and to copying songs for Magdalena.

Sebastian enjoyed trying his hand as a poet, and here
is another song by him from her notebook. This time it
is a comic verse, *Edifying Thoughts of a Tobacco Smoker.*
Everything about it—the homeliness, the unforced piety,
and the rough-and-tumble humor—reveals the author and
his attitude to life.

"Whene'er I take my pipe and stuff it
And smoke to pass the time away
My thoughts as I sit there and puff it
Dwell on a picture, sad and gray.
It teaches me that very like
Am I myself unto my pipe.
Like me this pipe so fragrant burning
Is made of naught but earth and clay;
To earth I too shall be returning.
It falls and e'er I'd think to say
It breaks in two before my eyes;
In store for *me* a like fate lies.
Thus o'er my pipe in contemplation
Of such things, I can constantly
Indulge in fruitful meditation.
And so, puffing contentedly
On land, on sea, at home, abroad
I smoke my pipe and worship God.

Six months went by, and still for various reasons the
Leipzig post was not filled.

"It would be the right life for you," Magdalena urged

"a great city, a center of church music, a famous song-school to direct, a university, and all the learned friends you lack here, where you have only me to talk to."

Sebastian struggled for a long time to make up his mind. When at last he came to a decision he pursued it with all the force and energy of his nature. "I cast my lot in the name of the Lord," he said, and from that moment he did not waver.

He presented himself in person at Leipzig and under-took to compose a work showing his skill in Church music. Within a few months he had completed the St. John Passion and on Good Friday he conducted it at St. Thomas's.

St. John's Gospel relates the Passion of our Lord with intense excitement and feeling. Sebastian read the Bible every day of his life, knew it thoroughly, and his response to its meaning shows in his music. The St. John Passion enacts Jesus's last days and death as a drama, in which singers, orchestra, and congregation all play their part. The evangelist sings the words of the Bible in passionate, almost violent recitative, and the soloists meditate like dissembodied souls upon the meaning of his story. Some of their arias are of unearthly loveliness, as when the bass dwells upon the sufferings and love of Jesus, to the throb-bing accompaniment of two lutes, regular and tender as a heartbeat. The choir takes the part of the crowd—rest-less, angry, with repeated shouts of "Crucify him!"—and a terrible, mocking court dances to the words "Hail, thou king of the Jews." The whole work is interwoven with chorales, which the congregation would be familiar with and able to sing, but which Bach has set with his own poignant harmonies.

It would be pleasant to write that the Leipzig Church Councillors were carried away by this magnificent music and appointed Sebastian at once. In fact they preferred two other candidates, and turned to him only when other negotiations had broken down.

"If one can't get the best musicians," said a worthy Councillor, sadly, "one must make do with a middling one."

Sebastian, on his side, was by now determined to have the post. He appeared in the Council Chamber before the row of desks and agreed not to make his music "too long or too theatrical."

"I express my most obedient thanks for the fact that you thought of me," he said, "and I promise my full loyalty and industry."

"May God's blessing rest upon the choice," said the pastor of St. Thomas's, and the councillors nodded their heads.

Sebastian even signed without misgiving the formidable document they presented to him, of which these are only a few clauses:

"I shall set the boys a shining example of an honest, retiring manner of life, serve the school industriously and instruct the boys conscientiously.

"I shall show to the Honorable and Most Wise Council all proper respect and obedience.

"I shall give due obedience to the Honorable Inspectors and directors of the School in each and every instruction.

"I shall treat the boys in a friendly manner and with

caution, but in case they do not wish to obey, chastise them with moderation.

"I shall faithfully attend to the instruction in the School and whatever else it befits me to do.

"I shall not go out of town without the permission of the Honorable Burgomaster."

The Leipzig Council wanted a model civil servant; instead they got a headstrong genius who was to plague them for years. Nevertheless the memory of his time there is the greatest glory their city can boast. And when Sebastian moved his household to Leipzig, it was the last move of his life. For twenty-seven years, until he died, he was to hold the title by which history knows him—the Cantor of St. Thomas's.

# CHAPTER ELEVEN

# THE CANTOR OF ST. THOMAS'S

## (1723-1729)

The stage coach from Cöthen lumbered through the western gate of Leipzig, and the Bach children craned out at the windows to see the avenue of lime trees and tall buildings which old prints show as the approach to the city.

"Look how wide the street is! There's room for two wagons to pass!"

"Catharina, Catharina, what is that picture of a black bear hanging over the street?"

"It is an inn sign, Bernhard. You must sit still and not point."

Fifteen-year-old Catharina settled her small brother firmly on the seat beside her.

"I can see another!" said Emmanuel. "It's the 'Wild Man'—and there's the 'Ostrich'!"

"And I can see the 'Three Swans' and the 'Red Oxen' —all in one street! How can there be enough people to drink so much beer!"

Anna Magdalena sat quietly, careful not to disturb the treasure she held upon her knees—her baby daughter Christiane, wrapped in miniature traveling cloak and

*The Bach family's arrival at Leipzig*

hood. She looked up at carved and painted houses, the window boxes filled with wallflowers and rosemary, the cages of linnets and nightingales. She watched the crowds pushing their way along, the apprentice boys shouting their masters' wares, the housewives returning from market, each followed by a servant with laden basket. She tried to imagine herself here, as one of these bustling citizens, after the quiet of Cöthen. The coach rolled on through the horse-market, and across the square past the turreted Town Hall. All around them rang the clatter of a town of thirty thousand people.

As the coach set them down, the children stood blinking and bewildered. Friedemann, at thirteen, was old enough to play the man of the family and order the postilion to

unload their boxes. Magdalena looked about and her heart
leaped with joy and gratitude. There was Sebastian, steady
and kind as always, waiting to meet them. She gave the
baby to Catharina and ran to kiss him.

Soon the family were looking at their new home. The
buildings stood on a wide cobbled square with a fountain
in the center. At one side was a massive church, with a
steep roof and a cupola. This was the great St. Thomas's.
The school stood at right angles to the church, a square,
whitewashed barracks with countless small windows and
a triple row of dormers in the roof. To their eyes it looked
huge and formidable.

"Are we going to live in that great house?" asked one
of the little ones.

Sebastian smiled. "Only in part of it," he said. He
pointed to a door at one end. "There is the Rector's lodging,
and there"—he pointed to the other end of the building
—"there is the Cantor's house."

The double doors in the center of the school were
flung open, and a procession of rough and tousled boys
poured out across the square to the church. They wore
uniforms—black cloaks and green caps—and the older ones,
who acted as prefects, were cuffing and pushing the
untidy line into some sort of order. In spite of their efforts
there was a good deal of scuffling and noise.

"There," said Sebastian a shade grimly, "there go my
singers, the St. Thomas's choir, and your future school-
mates, my sons!"

He led them to their own private door in the side of
the building. Anna Magdalena looked about her in the
narrow hall and staircase with a housewife's quick eye.

"Everything freshly scrubbed and whitewashed," she said. "That gladdens my heart to see."

Already the children had run ahead and were exploring the rooms. There was a ground-floor room looking onto the square, a smaller room behind, and a wash house with copper pots for boiling the linen.

"You boys will sleep down here," said Magdalena, but they were already running up the stairs, two at a time.

"Look, Mama, look how lovely it is from the back windows!" they called.

"This is the parlor," said Sebastian, as their parents followed. "Here I hope we shall have the joy of our family concerts in the evening. Here you shall sing to me, my dearest."

She gave a little cry of pleasure. The large room at the back of the house was lit by two windows, and the town ended so suddenly on this side that they looked out over open country. The river Pliesse, laced by many bridges, wound its leisurely way under the shade of willows and lime trees. Great mill wheels swung in the water, and the cool drops flying from their spokes made a perpetual freshness in the air.

"You will make music to the sound of the mill, like old Veit, Father," said Friedemann, for of course Sebastian had told his children the family legend of Miller Bach.

"Will the sound of the mill wheels disturb your work, my love?" asked Magdalena anxiously.

"Not so much as my neighbors will. Listen!"

He led her into the narrow little room next door, which was to be his "composing study." There was a confused shouting and thumping of feet on the far side of the

wall. "The boys of the youngest class have their class-
room there; and look, here is a door from our rooms di-
rectly into the school corridor. The school is above and
around us."

The rest of the house was soon seen—bedrooms, a narrow dining room, and a kitchen. There was no water
indoors. The family had to use a metal tub for bathing
in the wash house, and an earth closet without a drain,
but these were the commonplaces of eighteenth-century
life.

Soon Magdalena was directing the men who carried
up their few pieces of furniture: a wardrobe, a clothes press,
a dozen chairs of black leather, their beds, their dining
table, and Sebastian's desk. She arranged her copper
cooking pots on the shelves and carefully unwrapped the
pieces of silver that were her pride: the candlesticks,
the coffee pot large enough for the whole family, and the
salver which served on festive occasions. The only objects
of real value which the family possessed were Sebastian's
musical instruments, and they were carried into the parlor
under his own watchful eye. At his death he owned five
claviers, a spinet, violins, violas, cellos, and a lute.

It did not take long to engage a serving maid and to
make the simple household arrangements. By half-past-
eight in the morning, on June 1st, 1723, Sebastian was
ready for his formal introduction to his duties as Cantor.

The pastor of St. Thomas's Church and the masters
and the members of the Council gathered in the school
hall, with Sebastian sitting among them. There was a
sound of singing at the door, and the choristers entered
to the tune of a hymn. Sebastian listened carefully, and

found a good deal to criticize. The phrasing was ragged and some of the young voices were rough and harsh with strain.

"We must soon mend that," he thought to himself.

The Town Clerk rose, cleared his throat, and began:

"Whereas it has pleased God to call to his rest our late Cantor, the worshipful Council has appointed in his place Herr Johann Sebastian Bach, lately Kapellmeister to the princely court of Anhalt-Cöthen, being assured that he will show respect to his patrons, cultivate agreeable relations with his colleagues, and bring up his scholars in the fear and wisdom of God."

Pastor Weiss offered a prayer and formally "presented" the Cantor to his new colleagues. It was Sebastian's first introduction to the host of officials, each of them insistent upon his own importance, with whom he would have to deal for the rest of his life. Sebastian rose and bowed handsomely. "I declare my obligation to your worships, my patrons," he said, "and I assure you of my resolve to perform all my duty."

His work as Cantor could now begin.

The school of St. Thomas's had existed since 1212, and from then onwards its scholars had provided the music for the main churches of Leipzig. The foundationers were boys such as Sebastian had been at Lüneburg, earning their education by their good voices. They stayed on at school until they were twenty-one or two, to provide the tenors and basses of the choir.

Sebastian's keen eye and keener ear soon found that the School had fallen on bad days. The Rector was a man of 71, weak and incompetent. The buildings were old, dirty, and overcrowded, the boys neglected and wild. Three classes were taught at once in the dining hall, the boys were crammed two and three in a bed, and they lived, studied, and slept in dark dormitories which were partitioned into rough cubicles like horse stalls. A large part of the choir income came from singing at funerals and currenden, often in rain, storm, or snow. Sebastian noticed many prescriptions for cough syrup in the school physician's book. He also found some excellent singers in the group, and many who had poor voices or were quite untrained in music. At rehearsals the good musicians were overworked and exhausted, the others disobedient and rowdy.

Sebastian found the St. Thomas boys a sore trial, but reading their school rules now, one cannot wonder that they were rebellious. They led a hard life, as these extracts show.

RULE 10: The bell rings at 5 a.m. in summer and 6 a.m. in winter, when every scholar rises, washes, brushes his hair, and is ready at the quarter hour to attend prayers, bringing his Bible with him. Clothes, shoes, and linen must be clean and tidy. No lights may be used in the dormitories. Chamber pots must not be broken, nor their contents poured from the windows. The walls must not be disfigured with charcoal drawings or writing. Before retiring to rest, the lessons of the day should be recalled, with thanks to God for the knowledge acquired.

RULE 12: On Sundays the scholars assemble quietly and proceed to Church. Food may not be taken into Church.

Leaving Church without permission before the service is ended is punished with a birching.

RULE 14: The Calefactor rises before the others to heat the building, and rouses them by ringing a bell. He lights the lamps on walls and stairs and extinguishes them. He sees that windows and doors are shut, directs the sweepers and keeps a store of firewood and sawdust. After meals he removes the cloth and spoons and sweeps out the room. He must not allow his duties to impede his studies.

No wonder that boys treated in this spirit swore and fought.

A system so harsh towards the pupils was difficult for the staff as well. Sebastian's fixed stipend was only 100 thalers (about $75) a year, although his extra earnings at weddings and funerals brought it up to about $500. For this he had to supervise four choirs and direct the music of two churches. He was unwilling to teach Latin, so he had to find a substitute Latin master at his own expense. He had to control the unruly boys as they marched through the streets. Rehearsals, classes, church services, and meetings in the Rector's study broke up his days, so that he could never know the fulfilment of steady, uninterrupted work on his compositions.

Sebastian hated more than anything else the weeks when it was his turn to act as Inspector, supervising discipline at prayers, class, and meals and living with the boys in dormitory and refectory from five in the morning until eight at night. Magdalena roused him while it was still dark, and there was hardly time to say goodbye before he had to pass through the door into the upper corridor and a world of noise and brutality. For a sensitive man, with creative work filling his mind, it was almost unendurable.

The daily life of the Bach family was as hard as a laborer's. They were all up by five in summer, and at six by candlelight in winter. They had one large meal at 10 a.m., and supper at five. Only in the evenings could they enjoy the peace of their own fireside.

Sebastian was not only a genius but a born fighter, pushing his way with broad shoulders and obstinate jaw through a host of difficulties.

When pupils came to him complaining, or colleagues wrung their hands, he disposed of their protests in a few words. "Everything," he said, "has got to be possible."

Yet from this life of toil and worry Sebastian drew inspiration for his long series of *Church Cantatas* and for the *St. Matthew Passion*.

The city had never seen such a body of musicians as gathered in St. Thomas's Church on Good Friday 1729, for the Passiontide service. There were two orchestras, each of seventeen musicians, the best Sebastian could find. In the two separate organ galleries were two choirs, each of twelve singers, whom he had rehearsed patiently for weeks. Pupils, university students, his own sons, all threw themselves into this great act of creation. There must have been some at least of the people near him who knew that this was the climax of Sebastian's religious music.

The *St. Matthew Passion* is both the largest and the deepest of Bach's choral works, the fruit of months of labor and a lifetime of prayer. The exquisite copy which he made in his own hand with ruler, compass, and colored inks to adorn it, suggests the place it held in his own heart. As the first string chords vibrate and the voices soar upwards, the listener is drawn into the heart of a mystery where grief and joy are indivisible. The evangelist relates the story to an accompaniment of terrifying realism. The earthquake and the rending of the temple veil vibrate from the organ. Violin, cello, flute, and oboe join in turn with the voices to paint the scene with vivid tenderness.

The chorus acts a part in the drama, shouting "Barabas" in the court of Pilate or whispering the fearful question of the disciples, "Lord, is it I?" The voices sing again and again the tunes of Sebastian's beloved chorales, each time in new and poignant harmonies. At the end the whole passionate grief of the world fades into a serene elegy for double chorus and orchestra, as the body of Jesus is laid to rest in the tomb.

In this great work Sebastian's genius went its own way, and fulfilled its purposes, unharmed by the clamor of schoolboys or the malice of provincial busybodies. Below his dogged obstinacy and his outbursts of anger lay depths of spirit untroubled and serene. Sebastian, with all his faults—and what man is without them?—was one of those who walk with God.

The Leipzig congregation was puzzled by the *St. Matthew Passion,* which was unlike anything it had heard before. One pious old lady held up her hands in horror and cried, "God save us, 'tis surely an Opera-Comedy!"

# CHAPTER TWELVE

# DIRECTOR MUSICES

## (1723-1729)

If the cares of Sebastian's position at Leipzig lay in St. Thomas School, its glories lay within the massive walls and pillars of St. Thomas's Church. Here he could be what he always signed himself in letters, *Director Musices*, or Director *Chori Musici*, the fountainhead of church music in Leipzig. To fulfill this office, worthily, he was ready to shoulder a crushing burden of work, week in and week out, for years on end.

The Director was responsible for music in all the official churches of Leipzig, and had to provide four separate choirs each Sunday. Sebastian himself could be in only one place at a time, so he had to find and train three assistant conductors from the prefects.

He himself trained the first two choirs in the long rehearsal room at the back of the school, looking out, as his own parlor did, upon the river. There he taught them his own music, freshly copied by Magdalena's hand, and these two choirs sang alternately at St. Thomas's and St. Nicholas's. The best choir, called the "first Cantorei," went to each in turn. The services at both these churches were very long and elaborate. At six the three bells rang, at seven the candles were set upon the altar, and long before seven Cantor Bach was leading his black-cloaked choristers to their places in the gallery. A picture in an old hymnbook shows the crowded loft at St. Thomas's, the singers and the musicians bending over cellos and drums in their Sunday periwigs, the organist on his bench at the carved and gilded organ, and the conductor, in doctor's gown, beating time with a roll of music.

Before every school year Sebastian held auditions for choir scholarships, in the long music room which was his second home. He struck chords upon the clavier, and commanded each boy to sing in turn, encouraging the timid and testing the over-confident by shrewd questions. Every now and then he stopped to write notes which were always kind and fair.

"Winzer has a somewhat weak voice, and little proficiency as yet, but he should, if private practice is diligently maintained, become usable in time."

"Pezold of Auerbach, aged 14 years, has a fine voice and fair proficiency."

"Schmied of Bendleben in Thuringia, aged 19 years, has a fine tenor voice, and sings readily at sight. He hits the notes very prettily."

Sebastian had a constant struggle to keep up the quality of his choir, since the few boys who could really sing well left to earn more money in opera. Nothing made him

angrier than when the Council gave places to boys whom
he knew would be useless as singers.

In addition to training and conducting the choirs, Sebastian was responsible for the maintenance of the church
organs. This was work he loved and always carried out
with scrupulous thoroughness. He was often called away
from Leipzig to inspect the organs in other cities, and this
annoyed the Leipzig council, especially as he was too independent to ask their permission, like a schoolboy, every
time he left home.

His work as a private teacher of instrumental music,
conducting, and composition, went on through the years,
and his large family was always increased by the presence
in the house of one or two pupils. Sebastian was nearing
forty when he came to Leipzig, and his strong, kindly
nature welcomed these young strangers as additional sons
of the house. On their side, the best pupils looked up to
him with a love and respect that was almost worship.

Since Sebastian's excellence as a teacher was known,
towns which needed a Cantor, or courts which needed a
musician, often applied to him for his pupils, and his
time was consumed by the writing of letters like this:

"The bearer, Hr. Christoph Gottlob Wecker, has asked
me, the undersigned, to give him a testimonial concerning on the one hand the deportment he has shown in
this place, and on the other the knowledge he posses-
ses in *Musicis*. I can testify this much concerning him,
that his conduct has been such as to give full satisfaction, and that his knowledge in *Musicis* has made him
a very welcome guest everywhere, since he has a good

command of various instruments, and no less well can make himself heard vocaliter* Also he has been able to give creditable assistance in my church and other music; therefore I execute this testimonial with my own hand and leave the rest to him to prove to you.

Joh. Sebast. Bach."

This testimonial, one of many like it, was slipped in to a friendly letter to "*Mon Très Honoré Ami,* which ended with a postscript of Leipzig gossip in which we hear clearly Sebastian's own characteristic tone of voice:

"P.S. The latest is that the dear Lord has now also provided for honest Hr. Schott, organist of the New Church, and bestowed on him the post of Cantor in Gotha; wherefore he will say his farewells next week."

Herr Wecker was in fact not even a school pupil, but a law student at Leipzig University who had taken part in the music at St. Thomas's. Young musical friends like this one came and went constantly, and were always made welcome in Bach's household.

It is easy to picture the Cantor in his study at the end of the day. All his family has gone to bed, and he, with time at last to answer his letters, sits, writing and writing, while the last embers slip down in the grate.

The days were too short for Sebastian, because when he had finished teaching, conducting, planning. and writing, his greatest work was still to be done. Faith and

---

*"Vocaliter" was a favorite word with Sebastian. It is Latin for "vocally." See also the letter on page 121.

genius alike commanded him to create music for the worship of God. As the Christian year unrolled in the services of St. Thomas's Church, exquisite music poured from him, to honor each festival. The first Christmas at Leipzig gives some idea of his passionate inspiration. On each of the three feast days, he offered a new *Cantata,* and at Vespers a superb *Magnificat.* By New Year's Day he had another *Cantata* miraculously ready and rehearsed. A little while before the wife of a Leipzig official had died, and for this funeral of an unimportant woman, Sebastian produced a small masterpiece, the hauntingly lovely motet, *Jesu, Priceless Treasure.*

In all, Sebastian composed five sets of *Cantatas,* each of which covered all the Sundays and feast days of the Church's year. They were not concert pieces for performance. Each was in fact part of the service for the day, and drew its text from the appointed Gospel reading. The settings reveal how deeply and imaginatively Sebastian read the Gospels. Nearly all were written at Leipzig, and most of them during the earlier years of his Cantorship, when he can hardly have laid down his pen. The astonishing total is 295 *Cantatas,* of which 208 survive, each one fresh, individual, and completely satisfying. There is no trace in them of strain, hurry, or the irritations we know he suffered in his daily life. Bowed over his desk in the narrow "composing study," Sebastian shut out the nagging of his employers and the shouting of the sixth class on the other side of the wall. His ears opened only to heavenly music, and the *Cantatas* shaped themselves under his quill.

The *Cantatas* are perhaps the least known of Bach's

great music, to the general public, which knows him from concerts and phonograph records. A list of titles in themselves mean very little, although some are as splendid as the trumpet calls within their pages: *Sleepers, wake!, How lovely shines the Morning-star, God is my king, Christ lay in bonds of death, Tread in the way of faith, My glory is in Thee.* But to musicians this music has been endlessly satisfying, and they know it through and through, in dusty practice rooms, recording studios, and hushed, expectant churches. The *Cantatas* are a world in themselves, a world apart.

All this meant very little to the Consistorium, that council of worthy clergy, laymen, and lawyers which governed St. Thomas's. It is very difficult to blame them. They needed a schoolmaster and found themselves with a composer at the peak of his creative powers. A run-of-the-mill Cantor who kept good order in class and bowed every time he saw the burgomaster would have suited them much better than the fiery genius they had chosen. As the years passed, they found to their dismay that it was impossible to either manage or browbeat Cantor Bach. When his ideas conflicted with theirs, he had no intention of giving way.

The first open quarrel concerned his right to control the music at the University Church. Sebastian valued this, not only for the salary, which he needed, but for the pleasure of making music with intelligent young people and for the dignity of the Cantorship. Further, he was infuriated by the incompetent organist, called Gömer, who had been put in charge by the council. One day at rehearsal he was so exasperated that he tore off his wig and flung it at Gömer's head, shouting, "You should have been a cobbler, not an organist!"

In 1725 Sebastian wrote forcibly to the Elector of Saxony,* stating his case. The council, nettled, replied without letting him see their letter. Sebastian at once wrote to the Elector again.

> "Potent and most gracious sovereign,
>
> I beg a further favor, that your Majesty will be pleased to cause a copy of the University's reply to be communicated to me, and that no decision upon my cause be given, until I have had opportunity to comment on it. My observations shall be communicated without the least delay."

He got his copy of the document and part, though not all, of the rights which had been taken from his post of Cantor. The Leipzig authorities were surprised and annoyed. It was not long before they attempted a revenge.

In 1727 the wife of the Elector died, and a young aristocrat of the university arranged a memorial service. The really gifted and intelligent university students had fallen under the spell of Sebastian's genius, and naturally invited him to compose the music for the service, and conduct it in the University Church. The University Council at once drew up a legal document, stating that this was

---

*Liepzig was a self-governing city with its own council and burgomaster, but it was under the overlordship of one of the most powerful German princes, the Elector of Saxony, who had his seat at Dresden and later became elected King of Poland. It was a very bold step for a commoner like Sebastian Bach to approach a ruler of this status.

"purely a favor and not to set a precedent," which they ordered Sebastian to sign.

The university clerk who carried the paper presented himself at Sebastian's door. For an hour he argued and pleaded, in vain. The pledge was unjust, and Sebastian would not be forced to sign it. He marched to the door and pushed the unlucky official out, paper and all. With a slam of the heavy oak and a sign of exasperation he returned to the musical theme which was haunting his brain.

The council attacked again next year by denying the Cantor's right to choose the hymns in church. Sebastian replied in his usual determined but polite vein:

"I request you will protect me in the old practices concerning the hymns and their ordering. Wherefore I shall remain my life long, Most Distinguished Sirs,
                              Your Most Obedient,
                              Johann Sebastian Bach."

In 1729 the subject at issue was more serious. We have seen how carefully Sebastian auditioned and reported on new candidates for the choir. Yet when he handed his list to the council they admitted four candidates whom he rejected and one he had not even tested. Sebastian, harassed and overworked, was now burdened with five useless members of his choir. No wonder he lost his temper with them and with his employers. Every feast day dawned for him in a rush of anxiety as he ran here and there, calling on university students and his own sons to make up a reliable body of musicians. It is tragic to think that he can never have heard his lovely music worthily performed.

By 1730, the tension between Cantor and Council was at breaking point. There was a stormy council meeting at which Sebastian's behavior was discussed.

"He has not conducted himself as he should!" said a worthy councillor.

"Indeed not! He ought to teach the third and fourth classes as well as the seniors," said another.

"He allowed one of the choir prefects to go for a holiday without telling the burgomaster."

"Worse still," said the burgomaster, "he even went away himself without asking my permission!"

"Everything that has been said against the Cantor is true," said Court Councillor Lange. "He should be admonished and we could give his place to someone else."

"Not only does he do nothing," said Court Councillor Stege, "he will not even explain himself! A break will have to come sometime."

"We cannot reduce his salary," said prosperous Dr. Holzel, "but I propose we restrict his additional fees."

"Agreed," said the Syndic, "since Cantor Bach is *incorrigible*."

And the gray wigs nodded around the council table, in high satisfaction at their own wisdom.

"Agreed."

"Agreed."

"Agreed."

Not one voice spoke in defense of Sebastian; not one councillor remembered that a few months before their Cantor had given Leipzig the supreme work of his middle years, the *St. Matthew Passion*.

# CHAPTER THIRTEEN

# THE CHILDREN OF ANNA MAGDALENA

There was never much room to spare in the Cantor's lodging. Emmanuel, when he grew up, remembered that it was "like a beehive, humming with life."

The three boys crammed themselves, their books, and Friedemann's precious violin into the narrow ground-floor room, looking over St. Thomas's Square. When Anna Magdalena's warning cry, "Hurry, children, hurry, it has struck six o'clock!" drove them out in the morning, they had only to run out of their own front door, around the corner of the building, and in at the great doors of St. Thomas's School, just in time for prayers and singing practice. It was no use hoping that their father would let them off lightly if they were late. His sense of justice made him deal as sternly with them as with the other boys. In the evenings they came home to share the family supper, then to join in music-making and do their homework in their own room. Friedemann's exercise books were found in a wainscot cupboard there, more than a hundred years later, with his name, his Latin exercises, and his scribbled notes and drawings, just as he left them.

With all their capacity for hard work, the Bachs had a gift for enjoyment too. On summer days the boys would send Catharina to beg for them, "Please, Mama, a picnic by the river!"

Once out of the west gate of the city, they crossed the river and ran into the shady woods beyond. Overhead the bees murmured in the lime trees (the very name Leipzig means "lime"). The older children played hide-and-seek among the trees, and Christiane took her first tumbling steps around her parents as they lay upon the grass. Sebastian would throw off his black coat, as if he were throwing off all the cares of the Cantorship with it, and laugh again, the deep, hearty laugh of his boyhood.

Spring and autumn brought their pleasures too, in the great Easter and Michaelmas fairs which had been

*Leipzig Fair*

held in Leipzig since the Middle Ages. Then the streets behind the town hall were filled with tents and stalls and mysterious tilted carts, crowded as an Eastern bazaar. The boys defied school rules and rushed out to explore.

"Mama! I saw a man from Persia—brown, quite brown! He had carpets of red and blue, just like the windows in St. Thomas's Church!"

"Mama! There was a Russian, a fur dealer. He was wearing a tall hat made of sable fur!"

Even Bernhard, who was not yet ten, tried to escape to the stall where little men cut out in gingerbread lay spread in baskets. "Everyone at school goes there," he protested, "everyone, even the choir prefects!"

Anna Magdalena was constantly trying to make one thaler do the work of two and could not save much for shopping at the great fairs. The floorboards at the Cantor's lodging were scrubbed by her own hands, and were covered with rushes rather than silk carpets. Sebastian, for his part, had no use for luxuries. Even he, though, could not resist the booksellers' stalls, where he would linger and browse, coming home in the end with some stout calf volume under his arm—an illustrated Bible, a commentary on the Epistles, or once Geyer's *Time and Eternity*—to add to the collection in his study.

For his own entertainment Sebastian most enjoyed a trip to the Opera at Dresden. His serious mind could not quite regard it as music, but his robust sense of fun drew him in spite of himself.

"Well, Friedemann, what do you say? Shall we go to Dresden and hear their little tunes?" he used to ask, and then father and son would go off in high spirits on the

Dresden coach, to return next day humming the latest Italian airs.

Such treats were the more enjoyed for being rare in the Bach family.

The boys worked hard at St. Thomas's School, and soon Sebastian had the happiness of entering Friedemann's name as a future student at Leipzig University. In the St. Thomas's Choir they were his most trustworthy singers, and at home they seemed to learn music from the air they breathed.

Catharina was her stepmother's right hand in the crowded house. Together, with the help of a serving maid, they baked, brewed, scrubbed, and darned for a growing family. During the first eight years at Leipzig, Magdalena gave birth to a baby every year. While Christiane was still carried in her sister's arms, the first boy was born, a sturdy placid child called Gottfried, who lay strangely still in his cradle and stared incuriously at the ceiling. Christiane could hardly trot up and down the passages behind her mother when a second boy, Christian, followed. She was just beginning to talk and to copy the singing of the women at their housework when fever broke out among the boarders of the school. Within a few days she was dead.

Magdalena was heartbroken, and Sebastian suffered as much in her grief as his own. He turned, as always, to Luther for comfort, and read aloud to her what the reformer had written on the death of his own little daughter.

"Darling Lena, how happy you are now! You will arise again, and shine as a star, yea, as the sun. How strange it is to know so surely that she is at peace and happy, and yet for us to be so sad."

Magdalena took comfort when her next baby, Elizabeth, was born. She grew up, with the pet name of Liessgen, to be the darling of the family. Yet grief was never far from the Bach nursery. Next year a new-born baby, Andreas, died, and a year later the three-year-old Christian. No one in the early eighteenth century had any idea of the nature or causes of infectious disease. Overworked, neglected, and herded together like animals, the pupils of St. Thomas's were often ill. Sebastian and the older boys went freely from home to the pestilent schoolrooms and back again carrying the infection of the continuous epidemics with them. In 1728 another little girl was born, to die just as she reached the most charming age, and two more girls, each pathetically baptized Christiane after Magdalena's first child, died before their first birthday. Of Magdalena's first eight children, born before she was thirty, only Liessgen and Gottfried survived, and he was the cause of a new sorrow.

They noticed that he was slow to walk and to talk, and Magdalena watched with sharp anxiety for the love of music which was the family gift, but Gottfried only hummed tunelessly to himself. When he began to touch the clavier she hoped again, but he banged the keyboard idly, like any baby.

"He has talent," urged Emmanuel loyally. "It is just that somehow it does not seem to develop."

The neighbors knew better. "Poor Frau Cantor Bach," they said as they watched Gottfried aimlessly wandering in the Square, "that boy is an idiot—one of God's children." Soon the parents could no longer hide the truth from themselves. Gottfried was helpless and incurable. There was no more hope for him than for the children who had died. Sebastian's acceptance of suffering and death never failed, for it was part of his genius, but Magdalena, so gay and loving, must have suffered bitterly in her motherhood.

By the time he was forty-five Sebastian longed to leave Leipzig. In spite of the glorious music he had created there, it was the scene of too many family and professional troubles for his peace of mind. Sebastian's chief source of income, apart from his salary, was the fees paid for funeral music. "If the death rate is higher than *ordinaire-ment*," he wrote, "my *accidentia* increase in proportion, but Leipzig is a healthy place and for this last year I have received less than usual in funeral fees."

He wrote for advice to an old school friend of Lüneburg days, not mentioning his private griefs but describing the situation at St. Thomas's. He set it out in his own business-like way, under 1, 2, 3, and 4, saying quite frankly that the salary did not meet the high cost of living in Leipzig, and that he suffered from the council's action in stopping his extra fees. He goes on:

> "The authorities are very strange people with small love of music, so that I live under almost constant vexation, jealousy, and persecution, and I feel compelled, with God's help, to seek my fortune elsewhere."

Nothing came of this plan to move, because, as we shall see, things changed for the better at St. Thomas's;

but the letter is precious because it gives Sebastian's own picture of his family life.

"And now I must tell you something of my home circumstances. My first wife died at Cöthen and I have married again. Of my first marriage are living three sons and a daughter. My eldest son is a law student, and the other two are at school here, one in the *prima* class and the other in *secunda;* my eldest daughter is as yet unmarried. My children by my second wife are still young; the eldest boy is six. All my children are born musicians; from my own family I assure you I can arrange a concert *vocaliter* and *instrumentaliter.** My wife especially has a good clear soprano, and my eldest daughter joins in not so badly."

It is a happy picture. The boys' homework has been finished, Catharina has put the little ones to bed, and the last copper saucepan has been scoured and hung up in its place in the kitchen. Anna Magdelena, for a brief hour, is free from her labors: even the Cantor has put his endless copying aside. They push back the table and draw the black leather chairs into a half circle. This household, usually so frugal, is in holiday mood tonight; they put fresh logs into the crackling stove and set candles on music stand and mantel.

Love shines like the candlelight upon this family scene, as Sebastian's hands draw from the keyboard the dancing

---

*That is to say with voices or instruments. Sebastian's love of foreign words shows often, as here, in his letters. Compare the letter on page 109.

music of his *Italian Concerto,* or when the two women sing his lovely, flowing duets. Then Sebastian and his sons might form a string quartet with the father in his favorite place "in the middle of the harmony", or the boys might move the claviers together to play his Concertos for two and three harpsichords. Much of the chamber music we cherish now had its first performance in that fire-lit parlor at the back of St. Thomas's.

# CHAPTER FOURTEEN

# A NEW RECTOR

## (1730-1734)

While Sebastian was fighting the battles with the council which brought him almost to the point of resigning, the Rector, as the Headmaster of St. Thomas's was called, was slowly letting the reins of office slip from his tired old hands. In 1730 he died, leaving the school unruly, unhealthy, and disorganized as never before.

The masters and boys buzzed with gossip about whom his successor might be. Sebastian was indifferent.

"What is wrong here is beyond mortal hands to mend," he said. "Let them choose whom they will."

Then, one day, he suddenly came home with his old vigor and gusto.

"The new Rector has been chosen. It is my old friend from Weimar days, Matthias Gesner."

"Matthias Gesner! How often you have told me about him!" cried Magdalena. "He used to come and sit in the Duke's chapel to listen to you playing. Now we shall see— at last you will be honored as you deserve!"

The new Rector was hardly installed at St. Thomas's before he came to call on the Cantor. "My old friend, how good to see you!" he said, and, bowing courteously to Magdalena, "Frau Cantor Bach, I am your husband's admirer, and your devoted servant." Magdalena looked into a face of great charm, with kind eyes and a thoughtful half-smile playing around the mouth. The hand which raised her own to his lips was slender and delicate. Here, she knew, was a man after their own hearts.

All thought of leaving was forgotten; it was the beginning of Sebastian's happiest years in Leipzig. For once he had a colleague and a friend of quality to match his own.

Matthias Gesner was one of the first of the great German classical scholars. He loved Greece and Rome with an imaginative passion, and his lectures opened new worlds to the students who heard them. He was a born teacher as well as a scholar. He enjoyed the company of young people, and could strike from them the sparks of his own enthusiasm. Outside his work his great joy lay in music, and he was one of the few people who really appreciated Sebastian's genius as a composer during his lifetime. With his coming there was a change in the spirit of the school. He called the boys together in the dining hall, where benches were hastily pushed against the wall to squeeze them in.

"My dear boys," he said, "you are the members of a choir school. To praise Our Lord in music links you with the heavenly choirs above. It is a great privilege, and I expect you to be proud of it—even to give up some of your free time for the sake of making your music perfect. In everything musical you cannot do better than obey your Cantor. Watch his every sign and beat, for he is one of God's great musicians.

"Do this"—his kindly glance swept around the room and took in the crowd of ragged, dirty and half-starved children—"do this, and I will do all I can to make your schooldays happy."

The new headmaster was as good as his word. Although he was not strong in body, he had the strength of mind to shake the Council out of its complacency. He insisted on new rules, better conditions for the staff, and new buildings. Within a few months the Bach family, with all the other masters and boys, had moved to temporary lodgings in the town, and an army of builders set to work on the grim old barracks in St. Thomas's Square.

The masters forgot their quarrels and grievances and began for the first time to work together as a group. As for Sebastian, he felt new hope.

"Let me deal with the Council for you," said Gesner. "They only rouse your temper, and waste your time, which is absurd."

"If you can make them see that music has a place in the life of the school," said Sebastian, "I should be your servant forever."

"To begin with, it is ridiculous for a musician of your greatness to spend his time teaching Latin and Catechism," said the Rector. "I shall insist that you take no subject but music, and have more time for choir practice."

"The Council will complain that I do not do my duty," Sebastian warned him.

"Then I hereby make you responsible for the music at early morning service every day of the week, since the hours in God's house are precious to you. Take heart, my friend; you have your dear sons, your good pupils, and I heard last Sunday a boy with a beautiful soprano. Soon we shall have the choirs of St. Thomas's singing like choirs of angels."

Nothing could remove the deepest difficulties between Sebastian and his employers, but Gesner did a great deal to smooth his path. The boys in the choir noticed that their headmaster liked to come every day to rehearsals. He would sit quietly at the back of the room, eyes closed, listening intently, as they picked their way through the Cantor's rich Cantata, *Sing to the Lord a new song*, composed in honor of the Reformation anniversary. The choristers felt themselves valued, and so gave their best. As for Sebastian, his heart rejoiced, after years of slights and neglect, in the Rector's friendship.

Gesner never, to the end of his life, forgot Bach, or doubted his friend's genius. Years later, when he was quite an old man, he wrote his memories of Sebastian playing his organ and conducting among his muscians at Leipzig.

"His hands move in one direction, his feet with incredible speed in the other, yet the many sounds blend into one harmonious whole. One of them sounds at the top of the scale, another deep at the bottom and a third midway. Yet seated solitary amid these clashing sounds—stupendous task!—he can compel each voice to silence or keep them all going together . . .

". . . Could you but see him singing and playing his own parts, yet at the same time directing thirty or forty musicians at once, controlling this one with a nod, another by a stamp of the foot, a third with a warning finger, giving each time and tune. This one man alone can tell in a moment if anyone goes astray and keep all the musicians in order. Rhythm is in his every limb, his ear takes in all harmonies.

"... Truly Bach is thirty or forty players rolled into one."

Such intelligent appreciation released all of Sebastian's talents. The four years of Gesner's Rectorship were a time of unbroken creation for him. In 1731, the second of them, he made one of his ventures into print, and published six suites, or sets of dances, in every mood from the courtly to the gay. This collection of suites had the typically modest title *Klavierübung*, or "Keyboard-practice: Composed for Music lovers to refresh their spirits." Sebastian was delighted with the welcome it received from musicians, and this encouraged him to collect another volume, including the brilliant *Italian Concerto*, which he engraved and published four years later.

In 1733, Elector Augustus II of Saxony died, leaving the throne to his son Augustus III, who was a patron of music and the arts. During the period of Court mourning no anthems or cantatas were sung in the churches of Saxony, and so Sebastian had at last the chance of a little leisure. He employed it characteristically to compose one of his large-scale works, the *Mass in B Minor*.

Augustus III had become a Roman Catholic, and since Sebastian wished to dedicate the new work to him with a petition for post of Court Composer, he tactfully chose portions for the Mass which the Catholic and Lutheran churches held largely in common. The *B Minor Mass* does not have the tenderness of Bach's Passion music, but it has a tremendous impersonal beauty, like the architecture of a great cathedral. Sebastian read his Latin prayers and creed with the same intense imagination that he brought to the Bible. At *"descendit de coelis"* the strings make a superb downward swoop, at the *"et incarnatus est"* the Holy Spirit seems to hover above the waiting world, and in the magnificent *"Sanctus"* the singers "like Cherubim and Seraphim continually do cry" an echoing and re-echoing, "Holy, holy, holy."

A year later followed the *Christmas Oratorio,* which is not, strictly speaking, an oratorio, but a series of six cantatas on the birth of Christ. Musicians still turn to it at Christmas—perhaps above all to the lovely *Shepherds' Christmas Music,* in which we hear the woodwinds as shepherds piping on the hills of Bethlehem, while the violins fill the upper air with the sweep of great wings.

Sebastian was happy at this time not only in Gesner's friendship but in a new appointment which he had taken over in 1729. This was to direct a musical society of fifteen or twenty students from the University. This society, called the Collegium Musicum, was outside the University's authority, and the young men had invited Sebastian of their own accord to conduct their singing and playing. Every Wednesday evening in summer, at six o'clock promptly, Sebastian set off through the south gate for Zimmerman's beer garden, where an old windmill still lazily turned above the green walks and arbors. The students waited for him casually, sprawled upon benches and tables, rattling the lids of their beer mugs to summon the serving wench, or shouting one of the old drinking songs:

*Zimmerman's Beer Garden in Leipzig where Bach and
his students made music every Wednesday*

"Fear God and be holy,
Drink beer and be jolly;
Fear God and drain the pot
You'll be both holy and jolly I wot."

However, sight of the Cantor's stocky, blackcoated
figure turning in at the gate was an instant call to order.
The young men snatched up flutes or violins, or arranged
themselves, music in hand, to sing. However many windows they might break during Fair Week, they were
serious music lovers and respected their great conductor.

In winter the same group met on Wednesday after-

noons from two until four in the cozy warmth of Zimmerman's coffee house in the city. There strangers would
come and consume vast quantities of cakes and coffee to
hear the young musicians perform. Everyone noticed the
outstanding brilliance of Friedemann Bach, now in his
early twenties, who could play with the same finished elegance upon both clavier and strings. Emmanuel took
his place in the concerts too. He was left-handed, and
his father, with a wisdom rare at that time, had not
forced him to use his right hand for string playing. Instead
he had concentrated on keyboard instruments and at
eighteen he already promised to be one of the great
pianists of his day. Bernhard, a year younger, was an
accomplished all-round musician.

Sometimes the audience made its wishes known and
there were shouts of, "Cantor Bach! Cantor Bach to the
clavier."

Then Sebastian would take his place in the center of
the group, and improvise entrancingly and at length upon
any tunes suggested by the listeners. The visitors would
go away content, able to boast that they had heard "Bach
of Leipzig" perform in person. It must have been on a
gay and light-hearted afternoon like this that the audience
heard a first performance of the delicious *Coffee Cantata*.
Its plot was more topical than it sounds to us today, for
many German rulers had laws against coffee drinking,
and employed special police informers who were known
as "Coffee Smellers."

The curtain rises on Father Stick-in-the-Mud and
his pretty daughter, Lieschen—sung falsetto by a young
man. He orders her to give up coffee drinking, but she

resists with pleadings and a tremendous aria in the operatic style, "Oh, how good my coffee tastes!" She will give up her promenades, her fashionable crinoline, even the silver ribbon in her cap—but not coffee! Father Stick-in-the-Mud is in despair, when suddenly she relents. Yes, she will give up coffee on one condition—if he will find her a bridegroom. "Please, dear father, do it today!"

Stick-in-the-Mud rushes out to search for the happy man, and Leischen bursts into peals of laughter, saying, "I shall have it put in the marriage contract that I can drink coffee whenever I like!"

The audience could not resist either the shy humor or the music. "Who would think our good Cantor could be so frivolous," they said to each other as they applauded and called for more of Herr Zimmerman's fragrant brew.

Another great occasion at the Collegium Musicum was the visit of Augustus III to Leipzig in 1734. Cannons were fired from the barracks, every householder set a candle in his window, and six hundred students with torches gathered in the Market Square, where Sebastian's young musicians serenaded the Prince with *Evening Music with Trumpets and Drums*.

Sebastian composed a whole series of secular cantatas and chamber music for the Collegium Musicum, among it some of his gayest and most brilliant works. His nature enjoyed their youthful high spirits, their robust practical jokes and sense of fun, just as deeply as it needed daily worship at St. Thomas's.

These were happy years in the Bach home too. In 1732 the family returned to the school's new buildings, where two complete stories had been added, so that the boys were no longer herded together like animals. The Cantor's lodgings too had been enlarged into a healthy dwelling for a family, Their happiness was complete when Magdalena gave birth to Johann Christoph Friedrich, who grew and throve, and then, in Sebastian's fiftieth year, to a charming, lively, and intelligent boy, Johann Christian, who came to be the joy of his later life. Two little girls followed, so Sebastian and Magdalena, those most loving parents, never knew a house without young children.

The older ones were now leaving them to take their places in the world. In 1733 Friedemann carried all before him in a competition for the post of organist in Dresden. At the same time Emmanuel left home to study at the University of Frankfurt, where he supported himself almost entirely by giving clavier lessons. Three years later he found a position at the court of Frederick the Great of Prussia, where he was to stay for nearly thirty years. Bernhard went when he was only twenty to take the position which Sebastian had once held as organist at Mühlhausen. The young musician played with something of his father's fire. "If he goes on like this," said someone, "the congregation will be deaf."

Looking at his sons, Sebastian could well be proud. "Yes," he said, "my children are all born musicians."

# CHAPTER FIFTEEN

# THE BATTLE OF THE PREFECTS

## (1734-1738)

On an autumn day in 1734 Rector Gesner hurried round to the Bachs' apartments.

"My friends, I want you to be the first to congratulate me," he said, "just as you were the first to welcome me here. I have been appointed Professor at the new University of Göttingen."

Sebastian shook his friend's hand warmly; he knew how long he had wished for a university appointment. Magdalena's pleasure was overclouded by anxiety for her husband.

"Then you will leave us, Doctor Gesner," she said. "I wish you well, indeed, but oh, how I wish you could stay at St. Thomas's and be professor too! Sebastian has been so happy while you were here."

"Come, Magdalena," said Sebastian, "we must rejoice with our friend, and have faith in the future."

Yet even his stout heart was troubled at the thought of the changes to come.

The new Rector, who took office in 1734, was no stranger to the Bachs. Johann August Ernesti, although he was only twenty-seven, had already been vice-principal of St. Thomas's for some years. His spare figure, dressed in academic gown and bands, was familiar in St. Thomas's Square. His keen eye and sharp nose had penetrated every corner of the school, inspecting, reproving, and controlling. He had long been known as a young man with a promising future.

Now that the Rectorship was his, he made no secret of his plans for the school. "The time has come for a change at St. Thomas's," he said to his colleagues. "Our city fathers, perhaps, are hardly aware of it, but there has been a revolution in learning. The need now is for schools which give a *modern* education, with modern languages, history, geography and, above all, with science. I mean to make St. Thomas's an outstanding institute of learning."

He was right, of course, and his work, following upon Gesner's, carried the school triumphantly forward to its great days. Yet for this ambitious program of learning something had to be sacrificed, and there was little doubt what this would be.

"It is undignified," said Ernesti, frowning, "for our boys to sing in the street like beggars. Then, at funerals and weddings, what do they learn but drunkenness and idle ways? They should be in class, furthering their education."

The hours given to rehearsal were another source of vexation to the Rector. He held a confidential meeting in his study to discuss the problem.

"Our Cantor Bach is a worthy person," he said. "Yes, a worthy person indeed, pious and God-fearing, but why must he waste the boys' time? The music he writes is too lengthy, too complicated; he is always demanding a half hour here, an hour there, for extra rehearsals, 'because the choristers are not note-perfect.' The school timetable does not leave time to squander on inferior subjects, such as singing."

Ernesti swept out of his study, angry and impatient. As he crossed the dining hall, he saw one of Sebastian's choristers, now promoted to second violin, with his violin part propped up on the salt cellar for a little private practice. The sight exasperated the Rector.

"So you mean to be a beer-house fiddler, do you?" he snapped. "A fine use to make of your education at St. Thomas's!"

Word soon went round among the boys that the new headmaster had no use for music. Gottfried Krause, Sebastian's faithful choir prefect, came to him with a worried frown on his young face.

"It is difficult to control the young ones, Herr Cantor, if they feel that music simply does not matter. In rehearsals they will not pay attention, and in church they get up to all sorts of pranks."

"You must do your best with them, my dear boy," said Sebastian. "You have my serious command."

But after young Krause had gone, he paced up and down his study, struggling with his anger.

To Ernesti, Sebastian appeared old-fashioned and tedious. He was older, he had no university education, his clothes and manners were homely and provincial, his faith was simple and unquestioning, and he worked at music with the steady patience of a craftsman. All these, to the Rector, were signs of an intellectual inferior. Sebastian, on his side, detected Ernesti's intolerance and his complete lack of feeling for music. Any musician might have found it hard to work with such a headmaster. Sebastian found it impossible.

For the first two years both men made an effort to keep up appearances. Sebastian composed the music of a "joyful welcome" for the scholars to sing to their new headmaster. Ernesti stood godfather to Johann Christoph at his christening in 1733, and to Johann Christian in 1735. But they could not work in harmony, nor could they avoid each other. They met every day at prayers, every week at staff meetings. They lived next door to each other, and in rain or sunshine their paths crossed in St. Thomas's Square. Magdalena, as she went out with her shopping basket, encountered the Rector's chilly bow. Sebastian, his mind full of his latest Cantata as he tried to hurry the choristers over to the church, would catch the Rector's eye, looking coldly down from his window upon the disorderly crocodile. Tension between them grew, until it exploded into one of the most famous quarrels in history.

In July 1736, young Gottfried Krause came back from escorting the choir to a wedding, very worried.

"Herr Cantor, I apologize, I have been very foolish."

"What is the matter, Gottfried?" asked Sebastian kindly.

"The little boys made a noise in church. I told them to remember their duty, but they only laughed in my face. Then the congregation began to complain, and I was worried because I remembered your orders. At last I took the boys out, and threatened to cane the ring leader. He fought back at me, and I'm afraid I hit him harder than I meant to. I am sorry, Herr Cantor," finished Gottfried miserably, looking down at his boots.

"I am sure you meant no harm, my boy."

"No, but the child has complained to the Rector, and

he is very angry. He threatens to have me flogged before the whole school."

"What's that?" cried Sebastian angrily, starting up. "Leave me to deal with him, Gottfried. The dear God will not suffer the innocent to be punished. I shall tell the Rector the whole thing was my fault and you are not to blame. He cannot intend to disgrace you!"

But the Rector, when Sebastian confronted him, was adamant. "He shall be publicly flogged."

"Think what you are doing, Rector," Sebastian urged. "The fault, if fault there was, is mine. Krause is not a child; he is a young man of nearly twenty-two, faithful and honest in his duties. The shame of a public caning would be cruel to him."

The Rector only shook his head. Meanwhile in the Cantor's lodging, Magdalena did her best to comfort the almost weeping boy.

"It is not the pain I mind, but the disgrace!" he sobbed. "I could not bear it, I could not! I would rather run away."

Magdalena stroked his tousled head as if he had been one of her own children, but could think of few words of comfort. That night when the Inspector made the round of the dormitories, Gottfried Krause's bed was empty. He never returned to St. Thomas's, and Sebastian never forgot the vindictiveness of the Rector, who even impounded the boy's few belongings.

The question now was: who should replace him as choir prefect? Sebastian appointed a quiet steady boy, the son of a village blacksmith. The Rector instantly objected. "There is another boy, senior to him," he said. "Another Krause, Johann, and he should be First Prefect."

"But you remember, Herr Rector, that we discussed

him last winter. To begin with he is a drunken young dog, with many debts and a bad reputation. Furthermore he is not competent to direct the choir in my absence."

"Allow me to remind you, Herr Cantor, that it is my privilege as Rector to appoint the Prefects."

"Your pardon, Herr Rector, since it affects the music in school and church, the right of appointing choir prefects belongs to the Cantor alone."

Ernesti then appointed Johann Krause First Prefect. Sebastian deposed him, saying that the Cantor alone was master of music at St. Thomas's. Krause slipped out of the Cantor's door and made straight for the Rector's lodging, to repeat this rash remark.

Ernesti frowned thoughtfully. "Cantor Bach will see who is master here," he said.

The struggle for power between the two men was now open and unconcealed. It raged for the next two years, as bitterly as quarrels do in the closed world of a school or university. All Leipzig soon knew that the Rector and Cantor of St. Thomas's were not on speaking terms, that they passed one another in the square with icy stares or heads averted.

Sebastian wrote with great correctness to the city council. "Since the Rector's action is contrary to traditional custom, since it stands to the prejudice of my successors; and is hurtful to the interests of the choir, I cannot allow it to pass unchallenged."

He could not keep his actions as temperate as his words, although Magdalena begged him to be calm.

"Do not let them make you angry, my love," she pleaded. "If you let anger get the better of you, then you put yourself in the wrong." This, of course, was just what

Sebastian did. On Sunday morning he found Johann Krause in the choir gallery, put there by Ernesti to conduct hymns. His fury boiled over at the sight.

"Out, you dog!" he shouted, and bundled him down the gallery stairs.

The congregation turned around in their pews to watch the undignified scuffle, and Ernesti rushed out of the church to meet the Cantor.

"Mark my words, you will regret this," he said.

Sebastian's face was distorted with anger; he lost all sense of the consequences. "Let it cost what it will, I shall never give way!" he cried.

At Vespers the same disgraceful scenes were repeated, but now the rector had forbidden the choir to sing under anyone but Johann Krause. The service would have broken down, if Sebastian's devoted old pupil Krebs had not stepped out of the congregation to conduct the singing. As Inspector for the week, Sebastian had to take his supper with the boys that night, and was tormented by the nudging, winks, and sniggers with which they discussed the quarrels of their elders. The Bach rage broke out again and he drove a boy away from the table with shouts of abuse.

It was heartbreaking for a man of genius to waste his life in such an atmosphere. Sebastian again appealed to the Council. "The services are in danger of interruption, the music sung will be ruined, and the body of singers lose all its discipline, if the Rector undermines my authority with the boys." Ernesti, on his side, wrote accusing the Cantor of neglecting his duties, and, most unjustly, of accepting bribes.

The Council was in an awkward position. They could

see the justice of Sebastian's appeal, but they thought
highly of Ernesti and did not want to lose him. Following
the time-honored tradition of city councils, they did nothing, and hoped that matters would right themselves.
Months passed and Sebastian's life was poisoned by a
sense of injustice. However much he had lost his temper
at first, there was nothing petty or personal in his attitude
now. It was the harm to music which grieved him.

"We can't sing with Krause, Herr Cantor," said some
of the boys. "We can't follow the beat when he conducts.
He turns three/four time into four/four, and four/four into
three/four. We don't know where we are with him."

"Imagine that," said Sebastian bitterly as he reported
it to Magdalena. "What will he do when they attempt to
sing my music, in six or seven parts? What good to compose
music that will never be heard?" For once in his life
Sebastian lost heart even for composition, and refurbished
old choral works for the church festivals that year.

He wrote again to the council, claiming nothing for
himself, but everything for the Cantorship. "I earnestly
entreat you to instruct the scholars again to show me the
respect and obedience due to me, and so make it possible
for me to fulfil the duties of my position."

The council, true to form, did nothing, and the wretched
struggle continued, casting a gloom over the whole family.
Little Friedrich and Christian had few of the jolly romps
and picnics their older brothers had enjoyed. Instead they
were bundled out of the way and hushed because "Papa
was worried."

Magdalena, to her grief, saw her husband, so warm-
hearted and generous, withdraw bitterly from the life of

St. Thomas's and Leipzig into a world of his own. He ceased to conduct his rehearsals or teach his classes, and when he could not get away from the town, spent more and more time shut up in his study.

Sebastian had not given up the struggle when, late in 1736, a message came from Augustus III, at last appointing him Court Composer. Instantly he sat down to his desk and drew up a statement of his grievances, which he posted off to Dresden, "humbly but confidently appealing to your Majesty's august protection to release me from certain provocations that weigh upon me." The king came handsomely to the rescue of his official. In 1737 he ordered the Council of Leipzig to investigate Court Composer Bach's grievances, and a year later he visited Leipzig in person. Sebastian composed the festive music, which was performed with great pomp, and was afterwards admitted to kiss his sovereign's hand. The king himself intervened with the Council. A Cantor could be ignored, but a court composer was a man to be reckoned with. The Council hastily patched up an agreement and the battle of the Prefects petered out at last.

It had left its mark on Sebastian. His portrait, painted in the 1740s, shows a man of formidable power and stubbornness. His heavy jaw is set, his brow frowning. His face is lined by the disappointments and bitter fights of his life as Cantor. At fifty-five Sebastian Bach had become an elderly man.

# CHAPTER SIXTEEN

## "GENTLEMEN, OLD BACH IS HERE."

### (1738-1747)

For the next ten years the fame of "Bach of Leipzig" grew. He withdrew from musical life at St. Thomas's, only to become famous in the wider world outside. The story of his long struggle against the Rector and Council went the rounds of Germany, and recalled old tales of his imprisonment at Weimar, his defeat of Marchand, and his youthful defiance of the Town Council at Arnstadt.

He became one of the sights of the city. Citizens of Leipzig would point him out to strangers: "Look, there is our Thomas Cantor." The visitor saw a plain and sturdy old gentleman, who pushed back his wig on his forehead when it hindered his work, or picked up a score and held it close to his face, to peer at it through short-sighted eyes.

There were stories about him of the sort which gather round any famous man. Some dwelt on his love of puns, of how, for instance, he had said to the great organ-builder Silbermann, "You are well-named Silbermann, for your organs have a silver tone and thundering basses. Just keep on building them!" The citizen was always ready to tell his visitor the latest Bach joke.

"Have you heard this about our Thomas Cantor? Last week he went to an evening party where an amateur musician was playing on the harpsichord. When the amateur saw the great master come in, he jumped up and left off with a dissonant chord. Bach's ears were so offended that he pushed past his host who was coming to meet him, rushed to the harpsichord, and resolved the dissonance with an elegant finale. Only then would he turn around and make his bow of greeting! Now, would you believe that?"

The visitor, watching the sturdy figure in the old-fashioned black cloak, hardly knew whether to believe it or not. He only knew that he had seen one of the great men of the day.

Sebastian's fame, though widespread, was curiously limited. It was as a virtuoso performer on clavier and organ that his contemporaries knew him, and all the stories about him touch on this side of his genius. His glorious compositions, the great range of his musical thought, his passionate feeling and poetic imagination, passed almost unnoticed. Of the hundreds of Cantatas, so faithfully copied around the family dining table by Magdalena and the boys, only one saw print, and that was an early production of his Mühlhausen years. Sebastian never showed the slightest personal resentment at this neglect. He had created, and in creating found peace of heart, deeper than all his daily struggles. He was content to leave his works behind him and look forward serenely to approaching death.

After 1740 his great days of composing church music were over; the atmosphere at St. Thomas's was too hostile to inspiration. When the Town Clerk approached him with some fussy complaint about the music for Good Friday, Sebastian simply shrugged.

"It has always been done so before," he said. "However, if you forbid the passion music, I do not care. I get nothing from it anyway, and it is only a burden to me. Let it pass."

Sebastian now turned his energies, first to keyboard and organ compositions, and later to the intellectual problems of pure music.

He steadily revised and prepared his organ manuscripts for publication. Between 1740 and 1744 he collected the second volume of *Preludes and Fugues for the Well-Tempered Clavier*, with twenty-four new preludes and fugues. This volume, added to the collection composed in Cöthen, makes up the great work which musicians affectionately call "The Forty-Eight."

In 1742 he published a set of variations of a theme from Anna Magdalena's Notebook, which are known as the *Goldberg Variations*. A Count of the Court of Dresden, who was an invalid, employed a former pupil of Sebastian's named Goldberg to play the clavier to soothe his long, wakeful nights. He commissioned from Sebastian some music for Goldberg to play, and was so delighted with it that he sent 100 louis d'or as payment. Although we call the variations Goldberg's, and might well call them Bach's, the Count was convinced they belonged to him. "Play me one of my variations, Goldberg," he used to say.

These were quiet years at the Cantor's lodgings, unlike the great days of rehearsal for the *St. Matthew Passion*, when every bed in the house and every moment of the day were filled. The family consisted of Magdalena, now tired and aged beyond her years, but still young in spirit, Catharina, a spinster in her thirties, and Liessgen, who took poor Gottfried under her special protection. It was his habit to sit quietly in a corner, apparently contented, smiling sometimes, and nodding his head to the music of clavier or violin.

The four little ones grew up remote from the affairs of the elders. Like all Bach children they grew up in a world of music. Their first memories were of crawling among the legs of the five claviers, or fingering the shining body of the cello. Sometimes Papa, a distant and impressive figure, took one on his knee, and struck resounding chords upon the keyboard. Sometimes he would command one to sing a note or hum a scale, and then nod his head, as if satisfied. The two small boys, although they could not know it, were already entering upon their destiny as musicians.

The household was increased by a young cousin, Johann Elias Bach, who had come to Leipzig to study theology at the University. In return for board and lodging with the family, he acted as secretary to Sebastian and tutor to the little boys. He stayed for four years, during which his letters show respect and admiration for Sebastian, and a son's love for the gentle Magdalena.

Only when a visiting musician passed through Leipzig did the quiet house come to life again. Then the kitchen fire blazed up, and Catharina plucked geese until she sat knee-deep in soft white feathers. Magdalena polished the silver and Sebastian came out of his study to count the glasses set out on the long black table. When evening

came the guests sat down to dinner, and there were rowdy
jokes and much laughter. After dinner the table was pushed
back for one of those impromptu concerts, which were
still Sebastian's chief delight. When the watchman's rattle
told ten, and the guests went out into the streets of
Leipzig, lit with flickering lanterns, they told each other
in surprise that "the Great Bach is a jolly fellow after all!"

Sebastian allowed himself more holidays during these
years than ever before in his life, though a holiday for him
always meant work, since he could never keep away from
music and musicians. Every autumn he used to get out
his cocked hat, his heavy black cloak, and his favorite
fur-lined boots to protect his feet from the bitter cold
of the coach. In the market square he would climb aboard
the mail coach, and go off to Dresden to visit Friedemann,
to Naumburg to test an organ, or to see Emmanuel now
in distant Berlin. As the spire of St. Thomas's sank below
the horizon, he could feel his spirits rising like a schoolboy's. On these excursions he could forget the slights and
pinpricks of Leipzig. In the world outside he was a king
among musicians and a musician among kings.

Through Emmanuel, the Bach family was now con-
nected with the most powerful ruler in Germany. Frederick
the Great of Prussia had suffered a lonely and bitter
upbringing in his father's court at Berlin. His father, Fred-
derick William I, was a brutal miser, who half-starved and
beat his own children. Frederick was an intelligent boy
with an exquisite ear for music, who loved to read French
books and play upon the flute. The flute was broken, the
books thrown away, and the prince kicked and caned.
At eighteen he tried to escape; he was brought back and

his closest friend beheaded before his eyes. When he became king, at twenty-eight, in 1740, his will was hardened to steel, and his character warped for life. Nevertheless, through all his sufferings and his own misdeeds, he kept his love of music. He gathered a group of distinguished musicians around him in his elegant new Palace at Potsdam, and appointed Carl Phillip Emmanuel Bach his official accompanist. Emmanuel wrote that he "had the honor to accompany, alone at the harpsichord, the first flute solo that Frederick played as King."

Emmanuel liked his little joke, as his father did, and invented a riddle about the musicians at Potsdam which made even the King laugh. Frederick's flute teacher, Johann Quantz, had great influence at court, and Emmanuel asked, "What is the most terrifying animal in the world?"

The answer was, "Mrs. Quantz's pug dog. It is so fierce, it frightens Mrs. Quantz herself. Mr. Quantz is frightened of Mrs. Quantz, and he is feared by the greatest ruler of our time."

Sebastian was naturally drawn to this musical court, where his son had a foothold. In 1741 he visited Emmanuel at Berlin, but had to come back without seeing the King because Magdalena was dangerously ill. "Our most lovable Mama has been very ill for a week now," wrote Johann Elias anxiously. "From the violent throbbing of her pulse we fear a creeping fever or some other evil." Magdalena recovered, but remained very weak, and affairs of State were soon to cut off the household in Leipzig from Emmanuel in Berlin.

A young Empress, Maria Theresa, succeeded to the throne of Austria, and Frederick of Prussia saw a chance to enlarge his kingdom at her expense. In 1741 he invaded Silesia with an army of thirty thousand men. In 1744 he marched through Saxony. A year later the tide of war swept right up to the walls of Leipzig and the city was besieged by a Prussian army.

The lovely woods and water-meadows around were devastated by gun-carriage wheels, the smoke of burning villages drifted across the town, and the cannons roared through the mist. Magdalena's tender heart suffered with the sufferings of the people, and to raise their spirits Sebastian broke his musical silence with a powerful cantata, *Thou Prince of Peace*. In November the city fell. Prussian soldiers were quartered in the houses, robbing the citizens of food, drink, and money, until a peace treaty was signed and the troops withdrawn.

Sebastian was a man of his times; he got on with his work and ignored the quarrels of rulers as far as he could. Family feeling drew him to Berlin, for Emmanuel had married and his first grandson had been born there during the war. As soon as he could, in the spring of 1747, he set out once more for the Court of Frederick the Great.

The Berlin coach traveled by way of Halle, and there Friedemann joined his father. They sat side by side in family contentment, while the springless coach jolted beneath them and the green plain of East Germany unrolled itself outside the window. Friedemann was thirty-seven now and had just been appointed Director Musices at Halle, but to his father he was still a boy to be encouraged and cherished.

"Well, Friede, how goes it at Halle?" he smilingly asked.

"Well enough, Father," said Friedemann. "It is a dull

town after Dresden, to be sure. There we had the court and the theatre and the opera always at hand. In Halle, can you imagine, dancing and smoking are forbidden and the women all dress like nuns. But I think they value a good organist the more for that."

"It is better so, my son," said Sebastian. "Had my poor Bernhard lived in such a place, he might be with us still."

Bernhard Bach had led a wild life after he left home, had run away leaving his debts unpaid, and died tragically at twenty-four, without seeing his father again. Sebastian sighed at the thought, then smiled once more as he looked into Friedemann's handsome, rather petulant face. His hopes were still high for his favorite son.

From Berlin they traveled the fifteen miles to Potsdam, where Frederick the Great held court. Emmanuel's square honest face glowed with pleasure at seeing his father and brother again and exchanging news after so long.

"The king my master asks constantly for you, Father," he said. "If he takes kindly to you, then you are a made man. But beware of his humor—he loves a cruel jest."

"Are you happy at court, Emmanuel?" asked Friedemann, half-envious.

"To be happy at court, one must talk French and say the king is the greatest musician in Christendom," said Emmanuel shortly. "Ask him to put down his flute and listen to a fine German singer, and he will tell you he would as soon listen to the neighing of a horse. Still, my master is no mean musician, and if he values Father at his true worth then I will think him a good one."

Frederick the Great was a man of devouring energy. From three in the morning he was dictating the letters at which his four wretched secretaries toiled all day. In his household not a barrel of fish or a bottle of wine was touched without his personal order. He reviewed his guards each day, like a drill sergeant, in time of peace as well as in war. He transformed the palace and grounds of Potsdam from the loathed scenes of his boyhood to an elegant court in the French style. With all this, he found time to arrange and play a concert each evening before supper.

On Sunday May 7th, 1747, the royal musicians were in their places and the king was setting out music on their desks, when an officer of the court brought him the list of passengers from the Berlin coach. Frederick studied it closely, as he always did. Suddenly he gave a cry:

"Gentlemen, old Bach is here!"

The musicians gathered around, and footmen went scurrying to fetch the visitor. Freidemann and Emmanuel could describe the scene that followed to the end of their lives. Sebastian was hurried in, dusty and travel-stained from the coach, protesting his apologies that he had not had time to change into his black cantor's gown. He cut a shabby, provincial figure among the mirrored walls and gilt candlesticks, the painted cherubs and porcelain shepherdesses of the Palace. Yet, for once, the king forgot to mock and sneer at the outsider.

"Not at all, not at all," he said, waving aside Sebastian's apologies. "The Cantor of St. Thomas's is an adornment at any court." With the easy charm that was his to command, he led the old man from room to room. In the music room, with its long mirrors, green marble statues, and tortoiseshell music desk for the royal flutist, Sebastian was graciously invited, "Do my dear Cantor, do pray try my new Silbermann claviers."

Sebastian played upon each in turn, forgetting everything in the beauty of its tone, while the king and his musicians stood by, entranced. With a start he came back to himself and this strange, glittering room.

"One might dream the golden age of Music was beginning in Berlin," he said. "May I invite your Majesty's gracious hand to set me the subject for a fugue?"

Frederick played a neat little theme, and rose from the music stool with a trace of complacency in his smile. Sebastian sat at the clavier, serious and intent, too absorbed in the music for personal flattery. He played the subject, another responded to it, and a third. Frederick's theme appeared and disappeared, like a distant horseman seen in sunshine and shadow, now in the treble, now in the bass, now weaving between the two. In the end the astounded king heard a fugue with six voices improvised on the spot.

The following day Sebastian gave an organ recital in the garrison church, and in the evening again played before the king. In between times he kissed his new daughter and little grandson, or walked with his sons among the statues and artificial ruins of the park.

Who can tell what high hopes they had upon those walks? Perhaps at last, after years of poverty and hard work, a triumphant career would open before Sebastian. Perhaps he too could share in a golden age of music.

It was not to be. Frederick II was preoccupied with politics and the threat of war. Also he had inherited his father's meanness in money matters. Sebastian received

*Sebastian walking in the Park at Potsdam, with his sons
Friedemann and Emmanuel*

nothing from the royal treasury, though a gift of money would have done much to ease his last years. At the last moment the king pressed an agate snuff-box upon him, and it is generally thought that an agate snuff-box, found among Sebastian's possessions at his death, was the gift of the king, who was a notorious taker of Spanish snuff. So it was with this meager reward in his pocket that Sebastian rode back to Leipzig. Nevertheless he had had his triumph. For one moment he had stood upon the world's stage, the greatest man, had they but known it, of them all.

# CHAPTER SEVENTEEN

# DARKNESS AND LIGHT

## (1747-1750)

Sebastian was no sooner home and in the quiet of his own study, than he returned to the haunting tune of Frederick the Great. In spite of his great public success he felt he had not done justice to the "truly royal theme" which had come to him on his exciting visit. Within two months he had composed, engraved, and printed a set of elaborate variations, with an important part for the flute. These he sent to Berlin, under the title of *A Musical Offering*, with a letter in which the thoroughness of the craftsman peeps through the courtier's flattery.

> "I was not blind to the fact that because I could not study the theme, my performance was not adequate. I resolved therefore to give a right royal theme the treatment it deserves ... and that resolution I have carried through to the best of my ability."

It is pleasant to know that thirty years later Frederick could still sing by heart the theme which he had set "old Bach."

Life was quiet at the Cantor's lodging after the splend-

ors of Potsdam, but Sebastian could once again enjoy the
company of sons who were more than adequate musicians.
Friedrich and Christian were both in their teens now, the
elder a patient and thorough organist in the old Bach
tradition, the younger a lively boy, already dreaming
secretly of fame and wealth in far countries. He meant
to be a musician, of course—what else?—but not a musician
like Father! Christian knew better than to speak his
thoughts to the tired, but still formidable, master who
took him so firmly through the rules of thorough-bass and
counterpoint each morning.

Sebastian's own thoughts were turning more and more
to the pure science of music. After his return from Berlin
he was elected to a learned society "for the Promotion of
Musical Science." He offered the society a set of variations
to demonstrate the whole theory of composing in canon
form, and chose for his theme the Christmas Carol, *From
Heaven on high to Earth I come.* It was one of the tunes
he had loved fifty years ago, as a schoolboy tramping
through the snow and slush of Eisenach at the Christmas
currenden. Now, at the furthest limits of musical thought,
he returned to it with the simplicity of a child.

There is a deep, calm happiness about the music, as a
German scholar said, "like the gaze of an old man who
watches his grandchildren standing around their Christmas
tree, and recalls his own childhood." Sebastian was never
a romantic or sentimental man, but perhaps for one moment he remembered the gabled roofs of Eisenach and the
choirboy in the snow.

As a further gift to the Society, Sebastian presented,
according to the custom, his portrait, holding the canon

in one shapely, well-kept hand. Here is "old Bach" as
tradition remembers him, massive head dressed incongru-
ously in a curled gray wig, heavy features, resolute mouth.
His eyes have lost the profound and wondering gaze which
Anna Magdalena loved. Now when she saw him frown
with the effort of focusing, or rub impatiently at the red,
inflamed lids, her heart ached for him. Sebastian's sight
was beginning to fail.

He had taxed it for years, from his childhood when
he copied Christoph's manuscript by moonlight, through
years of performing and copying under the candle's wav-
ering flame. Now the lines of meticulous figures in his
household account began to topple as he looked at them,
and the notes of music whirled like a black snowstorm
across the page. He was as active, as impatient as ever;
brushing help aside, he struggled on alone.

Sebastian still had work to do, always more work.
In 1749 he began his last great composition, *The Art of
Fugue*. Like the *Musical Offering*, it is a set of contra-
puntal variations, all based on the same idea and in the
same key. The variations demonstrate and solve every
problem which can arise in the difficult art of writing a
fugue. Sebastian did not live to finish it, but even as it
stands it is one of the masterpieces of musical thought,
a fitting swan-song for a genius.

Family affairs still pressed hard upon him. With years
of frugal living and the most careful economy he had
still been able to save very little as a provision for his
family. Johann Elias, now married and settled, sent him
a cask of wine as a present, which was damaged and
spilled on the journey. Poor Sebastian lamented that "even

the least drop of this noble gift of God should have been spilled," but he could not afford another cask, even as a gift. "The carriage costs 16 groschen, the delivery man 2 groschen, the customs inspector 2 groschen, the inland duty 5 groschen 3 pfennig and the general duty 3 groschen, so my honored cousin can judge for himself that the present is really too expensive."

Counting the pennies was not enough. Sebastian had to give up the plan to send Friedrich to the university, and at eighteen the boy left home to earn his living as court musician to the Count of Bückeburg.

In 1749 the Bach family had a great festival, the marriage of Liessgen, first and only child to be married from their house. Young Herr Altnikol had been one of Sebastian's best pupils, from the time he first appeared as a university student in Leipzig. He could sing, play the organ and conduct, and he was so conscientious that Sebastian gave him the highest praise he could think of.

"He knows how to treat an organ well."

Magdalena, although unworldly, was no simpleton. She noticed that Altnikol always appeared early for his lessons and left late, and that Liessgen, fresh and laughing, always seemed to be on the staircase when he passed. Pretty Liessgen, like her namesake in the *Coffee Cantata*, knew how to deal with old Father Stick-in-the-mud. Soon Sebastian loved and trusted the young man, who came to take the place of his own sons, now far away. He loved him still more for loving Liessgen.

Sebastian had found young Altnikol a post as organist at Naumburg, and was welcoming him back to Leipzig as a future-son-in-law. It was a joy to take Liessgen on his arm as he had taken her mother, and walk her across the square to her wedding at St. Thomas's. The wedding breakfast was the last family party they were to hold, and after it the house seemed strangely empty with Liessgen and Friedrich gone.

A few months later Sebastian fell suddenly ill, and rumors began to fly round Leipzig.

"Cantor Bach has had a stroke!"

"He lies helpless on his bed and cannot move."

"The council has already appointed his successor!"

In fact the council, impatient to be rid of their troublesome servant, had already held a trial at the Inn of the Three Swans, for the "future position of Thomas Cantor, if the director musices should pass away."

Sebastian heard the shameful story; his fighting spirit, and for a moment his old wry humor, were roused.

"They have not done with me yet," he said.

Painfully he struggled from his bed, and with all the force of his tremendous will attacked his work again. For more than a year he fought on. Magdalena grieved to see him grope his way into the house he knew so well, or feel for the useless pen on his composing desk and throw it down in despair. Helpless and hopeless she watched his agony, as sight left him day by day.

For a moment there seemed to be hope. In the spring of 1750 his old friends came to him with good news.

"Herr Cantor, there has come to Leipzig a visiting Englishman, a marvelous oculist, the Chevalier Taylor, who has performed wonderful cures. An operation by him, and your sight may be restored!"

The operation was attempted in January 1750. It promised at first to be successful. Sebastian could still see the light, and guided by Christian's hand could feel his way up to the choir loft to direct his singers. He even attempted to revise his organ chorales, returning again and again to the splendid hymns he had sung all his life.

In July he had a sudden relapse, and the darkness closed around him. The iron constitution which had carried him through years of struggle and toil was failing now. He lay in his darkened room, knowing by ear alone all that went on around him. That shouting and the clatter of wooden shoes were the St. Thomas boys at play in the square. The regular clacking was the mill wheel, endlessly spinning in the river. The distant music was the organist practising in church for the next Sunday's Cantata. The soft footfall at his bedside was Magdalena, near, as he had asked her to be, in death.

He was able to speak, to ask for what he wanted.

"Liessgen—"

"I am here, Father, here beside you." Liessgen and Altnikol had come from Naumburg at the news of his collapse.

"Poor Gottfried—"

"Do not be anxious, Father, we will care for him."

"Son Altnikol—"

"I am here, sir, here at your side."

"Take pen and paper and sit by my bed."

Even now he struggled to work, dictating his last Chorale Preludes. Death had never seemed forbidding to him, and now it was more than ever his friend.

"Son Altnikol, take pen and paper and write thus:

Before Thy throne, oh God, I stand—
Myself, my all are in Thy hand;
Turn to me Thine approving face
Nor from me now withhold Thy grace.

Grant that my end may worthy be
And I may wake Thy face to see.
Thyself for evermore to know.
Amen, Amen, God grant it so!"

This was his last music. Next day for a few hours his sight returned; he could see the light on the great buttressed wall of St. Thomas's, and Magdalena's face bending over him. Then he had a second stroke, and lay unconscious for ten days.

On July 28th, 1750, the pastor of St. Thomas's made an announcement from his pulpit:

"The right worthy and esteemed Johann Sebastian Bach, Composer to his Majesty and Cantor of St. Thomas's School, has passed to his rest and now sleeps blessedly in God."

# CHAPTER EIGHTEEN

# THE END OF THE STORY

## 1. THE FAMILY

With Sebastian's death the old close family circle of the Bachs broke up. There were no more family parties, no riding from one little Thuringian town to another for prayers and a quodlibet. Sebastian's sons traveled far from their old home.

Friedemann left Halle and drifted to Berlin, where he struggled for years against poverty and illness. This most talented of Bach sons had none of his father's indomitable spirit. Gradually he was reduced to shabby shifts to earn a living, copying his father's music and passing it off as his own. Gossip even said, probably untruthfully, that his brother once recognized him in a band of street musicians. Friedemann died, lonely and embittered, in 1784.

With Emmanuel we return to the old Bach virtues. He had his father's inquiring mind, his business sense, his utter reliability. It was he who, at Sebastian's death, followed the family tradition by giving a home and an excellent musical education to his young half-brother Christian. He sent money to help poor Gottfried and Elizabeth, when her husband died. He even attempted the difficult task of helping Friedemann. He was the keeper of family treasures, his father's portraits, his manuscripts, and the old picture of Hans Bach "the Jester", which generations of Bach children had loved. Nicolaus Forkel, Sebastian's first biographer, turned to him for help, and though Friedemann also contributed information, most of our knowledge of his great father comes from Emmanuel's love and loyalty. In middle age he moved to Hamburg as director musices. When he died in 1788 he was far better known as a composer than ever Sebastian had been.

Friedrich was the only one of the brothers who lived his life according to the old family pattern. At eighteen he settled in the little town of Bückeburg, among the lovely beech forests of Westphalia, and stayed there, making music, for the rest of his life. He was always poor and never famous, but his compositions have a depth and seriousness worthy of his name. In all life's troubles, like his father, he turned to music, and was still hard at work when death overtook him in 1795.

Sebastian's youngest son had the strangest history. Christian, "the English Bach", set out for fame and success. He had all the family talent and resource, with a worldly charm quite foreign to the Bachs. Most probably the charm, like his dark-eyed good looks, came from Magdalena. At the age of twenty he broke away from the family and went to Italy, where he studied opera, called himself Giovanni and joined the Roman Catholic Church. He traveled to England, became "Mr. John Bach, a Saxon Professor," music master to the Queen, and a leading composer and impresario of the London opera. He led a life contrary to everything in the family tradition, of dazzling success, luxury and large debts. He died early, in 1782, and all his property had to be sold to pay tradesmen's bills.

The story of Sebastian's widow and daughters is sad. For years he had worked, economized and argued with his employers to save money for them to live on. Magdalena, through all the twenty-nine years of her marriage, had toiled without ceasing for her large family. This lifetime of effort was not enough to save her from want when the estate was divided among nine surviving children. After sharing the life of a good and great man, she refused to think of marrying again. She would rather live quietly in Leipzig with Catharina and the two little girls, aged thirteen and eight. The Council gave her a half-year's salary and notice to quit the house which had been home for so long. She found lodgings and began the long struggle to make ends meet. One by one she was forced to sell her possessions with all the memories that surrounded them—the silver coffee-pot, the salt cellars, the copper saucepans she had scoured and burnished every day; even Sebastian's music. Her own sons were too young to help her, her stepsons too far away in a country divided by the wars of Frederick the Great.* At last there was nothing left for Sebastian's "beloved" but to live on a dole from the Leipzig authorities. When death released her in 1760 they gave her a pauper's funeral.

The last we hear of Sebastian's children is in 1800.

---

*The Seven Years War between Prussia and Austria broke out in 1756 and Leipzig became enemy territory for residents in Westphalia, Halle, or Berlin. It was difficult to send or receive letters, and money would certainly not have gotten through.

By then they had all died except the youngest, Susanna, who could remember the figure of her father at the harpsichord in the long supper room at the Cantor's lodging, as a dream lost in the mists of fifty years. Now she was getting old, too ill to work, too proud to beg. A fund was opened to save her from starving. Susanna wrote a letter of thanks to her helpers, which is pathetic in its gratitude and family feeling. "If it is granted to the spirits of my father and brothers to sympathize in what befalls me," she wrote, "how must their past compassion be turned into joyful sympathy with my happiness."

It is the last word from the Bach family circle.

## 2. THE MUSIC

For a generation after his death Bach's music lived only in the memory of a few faithful friends and pupils. His sons, as long as they lived, played his clavier and organ music, but only a small circle of listeners gathered to admire the tremendous architecture of his style. Already in Sebastian's lifetime, musical taste was changing. The amateur of the eighteenth century, elegantly dressed in watered-silk coat and powdered wig to match his rococo music room, did not want to fatigue his brain with the balanced complexities of counterpoint. He wanted a graceful melody in the Italian style, with an airy accompaniment which set his satin slipper tapping to its own regular beat.

"Old Bach? A barbarian!"

The lovely suites and concertos were put away, and the latest works of Pergolesi or Alberti took their place on the music stand.

In the choir gallery at St. Thomas's, the exacting scores of Bach's Passions and Cantatas were thankfully rolled up. At last on Sundays the Leipzig councillors heard something they could understand; the choirboys, released from hours of practice, ran joyfully to hopscotch and marbles in the square outside.

By 1756 only thirty copies of the great *Art of Fugue* had been sold. By 1780 Sebastian was known only as the father of Carl Phillip Emmanuel and the fashionable Johann Christian.

It was easy for Bach's successors to overlook his genius, since his great intellectual powers went with such personal modesty. He did not claim to be inspired, a man set apart, but simply to be a musician composing as part of his professional duties, and offering his work in humble faith to his God. His life was unswervingly dedicated to his art from the night he copied the precious manuscript by moonlight, until almost the day of his death. German chorales, Italian airs, and French dances all served his purpose. He accepted everything in music which rang true, and made it his own by profound and original thought. In oratorio, cantata, and motel for choir, in suite and concerto grosso for orchestra, in a whole range of works for organ and clavier, he demonstrated to perfection the art and science of polyphony. Bach was content to live his earthly life within a narrow round, but his music cannot be contained in any one country or period. It contains within itself the past and the future, the eternal life of great art.

It took a genius to recognize the genius of Bach. In 1789 Mozart visited Leipzig, and Doles, the organist of St.

Thomas's, who appreciated his great predecessor, trained the choir to sing the double-chorus, *Sing to the Lord a new song*. Mozart had never heard any of Bach's unpublished choral music, since copies were rare. At the first bars he sat up, startled. "What is this?" he called, then fell silent and still.

"All his soul seemed to be in his ears," said the friend beside him.

After the singing he questioned Doles. "Can I see the score? Now there is something one can really learn from!"

"I have not a full score," said the organist, "but I could show you the separate parts. We keep a collection of all Bach's motets."

"That's fine! Let's see them." Mozart was excited quite out of his usual gentle manner. He sat down in a pew, with parts in both hands, on his knees, and all around him. He forgot his surroundings, his appointments, everything in the world but the music he was reading.

After that one begins to hear of Bach again. A gentleman in Bonn went to a concert by a child prodigy, a dark boy of eleven who played his way with passionate concentration through the *Well-Tempered Clavier*. This child was Ludwig van Beethoven. Beethoven grew up and went to seek his fortune in Vienna. There he used to go for an evening's music-making with a patron, whom he could never leave "without half a dozen fugues by Bach as a final prayer." Beethoven shared Sebastian's love of puns, and used to say as he closed the piano for the night, "Yes, his name should not be Bach (brook) but Meer (ocean)." Although he was often harassed by money troubles himself, he helped to collect the fund for Susanna Bach, in memory of her great father.

Meanwhile Forkel was collecting materials for a biography of Bach. Friedemann and Emmanuel told him everything they could remember, from the stories Sebastian told of his own childhood to their memories of his last days. They produced letters, pictures, copies of music, and "never spoke of their father's genius without love and reverence."

When Forkel's biography came out in 1802, it was worthy of its subject. People, as they read it, felt like the English organist, Dr. Wesley. "It appears by the life of Sebastian, he was not only the greatest Master, but also one of the most worthy and amiable characters that ever adorned Society. I remember often exclaiming when working at him, 'I am sure that none but a *good* man could have written thus'; and you perceive that my conjecture was accurate."

Meanwhile a new generation of musicians was growing up, eager to discover and explore the beauties of Bach. In the 1820s young Felix Mendelssohn, son of a wealthy and cultured banker in Berlin, used to go with his sister Fanny to a choral society at the house of the conductor Zelter, where they sometimes studied the Cantatas. Zelter was a collector of rare Bach manuscripts, who would sometimes jealously show his treasures to the Mendelssohns.

Felix became obsessed with the desire to study and own the great *St. Matthew Passion,* and at Christmas 1823 his grandmother had a copy made for him as a present. He began to practice it with his singing friends, and a new world opened to the young people as they grasped it piece by piece. Why not perform this masterpiece which had lain forgotten for nearly a century? Felix pondered the difficulties. "If I were sure I could carry it through, I would. Anything for the honor of God and Sebastian Bach!"

The arrangements took years, the rehearsals months more, Felix conducting with the inflexible perfection of a great musician, and meeting all difficulties with his own tact and charm. In March 1829 he conducted the first public performance in a hundred years of the *St. Matthew Passion.*

It was a revolution in the history of music. "No one ever suspected old Bach of all this!" said a musician, overwhelmed by the beauty and passion of the drama. From that performance the modern cult of Bach began.

Felix was now helped by a friend, the young composer and writer on music, Robert Schumann. Schumann, who followed his own advice—"Let the *Well-Tempered Clavier* be your daily bread"—at once saw the need for a complete edition of Bach's works. This was the only way to preserve his music and his fame for all generations to come. "Do not think," urged Schumann, "that old music is old-fashioned. A beautiful true word can never be out-of-date, nor can a beautiful piece of true music."

In 1850, a hundred years after Sebastian had been quietly buried in the town graveyard, Schumann helped to found the Bach Society at Leipzig. The aim of the society was to publish Bach's works, complete and unaltered, as he left them. For fifty years the society went steadily about its work. The great organist, Dr. Albert Schweitzer, when he was 80 years old, still remembered his joy as a student, whenever one of the tall gray volumes of the Bach Society Edition arrived. By 1900 the publication was complete. The treasure house of Bach's music, in forty-six volumes, was open to all musicians forever.

A musician should have the last word. Schumann, who knew Sebastian's music to the depths, chose these words to describe him: "Bach was a man, out and out. With him, nothing is half done: everything is written as if for eternity."

# INDEX